So You Think You Want To Retire

Now What?

Robert M. Couch

Copyright © 2018 Robert M. Couch

ISBN: 978-1-7188-3155-1

All rights reserved. No part of this book may be reproduced or transmitted in any form or by any electronic or mechanical means, including information storage or retrieval systems, without written permission of the publisher.

Table of Contents

Acknowledgments.................................... 4
Preface.. 5

Part I—Establishing the Rules..................... 13

  1. Why Are You Reading This?....................... 15
  2. Just Do What Makes You Happy.................... 21
  3. I'm Driving Me Crazy............................ 41
  4. Spirituality................................... 49
  5. I've Got Friends in Flow Places................. 55
  6. Oh No! Not Another Infomercial About Exercise... 63
  7. Have You Heard the One About.................... 67
  8. Resilience, or No Excuses....................... 73
  9. Pulling It All Together......................... 83

Part II—Applying the Rules........................ 93

  10. Heading for Hayden............................. 95
  11. Heading for Harbert............................ 117
  12. Heading for Hoover............................. 141
  13. Heading for Hoover—the Sequel.................. 161
  14. Heading for Hell (and Back)—Bookus Interruptus.. 167
  15. Heading for Hoover—the Sequel (continued)...... 175
  16. Heading for Hemingway's House................... 195

Epilogue... 203
Appendix... 207
End Notes.. 209
About the Author................................... 217

Acknowledgments

Many people helped make this book a reality. Naturally, singling out any of them risks offending any I omit, but I'm up to the challenge.

First, my editor Susan Alison has patiently worked with me to sand off the rough edges of my manuscript. She gets no blame for any inaccuracies in the content, but she deserves much credit for making sure that I didn't make blatant errors of syntax.

Several people looked at early drafts of the book and provided me encouragement to proceed. In that category I include my friends Bill Terry, Brandy Hydrick, and Perry Hooks. I suppose their crimes fall in a broad category of aiding and abetting.

I owe a special form of combat tribute to those friends and family who helped me develop and deliver my Stardome stand-up comedy routine. Some of them weathered the early versions and, at least, acted amused. Others made the trek to Hoover, Alabama, to hear one of the live performances. All created a debt that I will struggle to repay.

For the rest of the characters who took this literary voyage with me, either expressly by name or implicitly by participation in my field research conducted for Part II, thank you. Your role was indispensable.

Finally, thanks upon thanks go to my wife, Anne. She designed the extraordinary cover of this book, but more importantly she willingly puts up with all of this, and other, nonsense.

Preface

As I sit here looking down the barrel of my 60th birthday and wondering how in the world I'm going to handle the next phase of life, I am reminded of the immortal words of Otter in *Animal House* in response to the question of how to deal with seemingly insurmountable challenges: "Road trip!"

Come along with me on an adventure. Admittedly, I'm a good ways into it, but I suspect you will have already seen some of the attractions before or you may have been curious about the terrain and you may have glanced at some of the travel guides. My hope is that you may be able to benefit from some of the packing and preliminary steps I have taken and, as a result, make better use of your limited travel time or, better yet, skip the line altogether and jump right on the roller coaster.

The journey I am taking is through mid-life and beyond. To borrow a phrase from Star Trek, to explore the final frontier. We are fortunate to have arrived at this jumping-off point and to be able to consider what comes next. We all have friends and relatives who have not made it this far. We have others in our lives who are not inclined to plan for the next stage of life. They would prefer to just "keep doing what I'm doing" or "take it as it comes." In fact, for economic or familial reasons, they may not have the luxury of being able to chart a course. Their boats are being driven by the winds of life and will be forced, at least for the time being, to continue a haphazard course and hope to stay afloat.

I am hoping to take a different path. None of us is in total control of our destiny. But we each have some capacity to influence the direction we are headed. We can't determine with complete accuracy the length of the trip, but we can increase the odds that the trip will be longer and in more temperate climes. It is my hope that with a little bit of thought and effort, the next stretch of the sojourn will be the most enjoyable yet.

This effort began in earnest several years ago. I was in my mid-50s and stumbling into a new stage. My wife and I had raised our children and had returned to

Birmingham, Alabama, after a three-year stint in Washington, D.C., engaged in public service. We were looking at an empty nest—and I was looking at the next phase of a career as a lawyer and wondering if I would ever retire. A close friend, for whatever reason (we had never discussed the topic of retirement), gave me a book that he had recently finished, *Younger Next Year*. He confessed that he had been intrigued by some of the issues it had raised.

I was finishing another read and dove into his gift to me. The thesis of the book is that we should all take a fresh approach to our "golden years." The authors maintain that, given current life expectancies and standard retirement ages, most of us can expect to have roughly a third of our lives ahead of us AFTER retirement. As such, we should all be careful to do what we can to make the final chapter enjoyable. Instead of taking the traditional rocking chair image of life-after-career, retirement gives us an opportunity, in fact, a need, to re-engage. In the authors' view, everyone has an opportunity to improve his or her quality of life by taking a few "simple" steps, such as regular exercise and a healthy diet. And then use the newfound energy to take on the next stage of life with a vengeance.

Younger Next Year examines contemporary studies to add another element to enjoying the next stage of life—to be purpose driven by something about which you have a passion. The book includes as one of its seven rules for healthy living the simple admonition that you must "commit and care." One of the author's pieces of advice is, unlike in his case, you should think about this BEFORE you retire, so you don't drift. By taking some post-retirement lifestyle plans pre-retirement, you find your moorings and are more apt to make the next phase more fulfilling after you leave work. This planning phase may necessarily include adopting (and adapting to) some of the activities that you hope will fully replace the forty to sixty hours a week that you currently devote to your career.

Upon reading this, I, like the author, was struck by the uncomfortable reality that I had no passionate pursuit to pursue. I had devoted most of my waking hours for the past 35 years to work and attempting to be successful in my field. What spare time I had, for the bulk of the period, was spent in my role as secondary caregiver to my two daughters as they grew up. Fortunately their mother chose to (a) take the primary role and (b) stay married to me for the whole time. And as with so many of us in the "sandwich" generation, I needed to devote some time to helping aging parents. Now that I had started to think about life after work, I began to pay more attention to the topic and I learned that there was a lot more to learn.

The thought that I was grossly unprepared to move beyond my vocation launched me on a process to identify suitable passions. Over the course of about a year, I had dozens of conversations with people I knew who seemed to be happy in their post-career worlds. I quizzed others who seemed to have ardent pursuits outside of the office. I also talked with a number of folks who counsel companies and their employees on identifying strengths and the pursuit of professional opportunities.

The evolution of this process resulted in a compilation of over 75 ideas for me to consider, ranging from treasure hunter to stand-up comedian. This led to a process of establishing criteria for narrowing the list, including seeking the input of my wife, realizing that she knows my personality better than I do myself. Fairly quickly the list was separated into two categories: possible passions and interesting distractions. Through applying some simple rules (e.g., genuine interest, perceived level of enjoyment, whether it would be compatible with a happy marriage), I managed to narrow the list to the top 12. Further narrowing required a good deal of introspection.

I soon realized that a critical piece of the puzzle is my own personality. It would be silly to settle on a course of action that runs counter to my interests and skill set. It would be a waste not to play on my natural-born strengths and talents. I also needed to be brutally honest about my shortcomings. (My wife nixed flying lessons due to my short attention span.) On several occasions over the years, I had undergone testing by various human resources departments and industrial psychologists to determine ability for and compatibility with various work environments. I dug through my files and found the results of most of those tests, giving me some insight into my personality traits.

While this exercise gave me some direction, I quickly concluded that the insights I was seeking now differed materially from the desired outcomes from the previous projects. I needed to consult a more current and relevant barometer. I came to the realization that virtually every business and nonprofit with which I have been affiliated for the past 30 years has undertaken a periodic planning process. Nearly all of those processes started with some form of a SWOT analysis through which the management or board undertakes to catalog the strengths, weaknesses, opportunities, and threats to the organization. Why not apply that same discipline to the personal planning arena?

I embarked on this step, which, remarkably, took more than six months to complete but also led me to another realization: It is one thing to come to grips with all of your personality assets, shortcomings, and predilections, but also you need to understand what solution you are seeking. This "aha" moment caused me to pause the process. What was I hoping to accomplish? To make the most out of my midlife and "plus" years, I want to increase to the greatest extent possible the likelihood that I would be happy. That sentence is much more complicated, it turns out, than it seems on its face.

What is "happiness"? And more specifically, what does the term mean when you are in your 60s, 70s, and up? How do we best prepare now for the changes that are likely to come, and, particularly, those changes that we dread most, such as physical infirmity and senility? Is it really happiness we should be seeking, or something else—contentment? Self-satisfaction? Well-being?

The more I thought about these questions, the more poking around I did on the topic and the more I became aware that while I was working hard as a lawyer/banker/government functionary, an entire field had developed, offering to provide answers to these pressing issues. This discipline is generally known as "positive psychology" and focuses on psychological well-being, or as put in the simplest vernacular—happiness. As I read more and more of the current scholarship on happiness, a few patterns began to appear.

True happiness is much more than a momentary feel-good sensation. It is more akin to overall satisfaction with one's life, and it requires a good deal of effort. The best example of this point is an outlandish one. Studies show that winning the lottery, while it is a common, everyday dream, will provide short-term happiness and long-term bitterness. In contrast, some of the conditions that produce the most sustained feelings of happiness may be decades in the making, such as raising a family.

Okay, so we want to lead a long, truly happy life. What else? When you pose the question to folks who are facing the golden years, you regularly get the "I don't want my body to outlive my mind" response. (You rarely hear the converse. I guess we have been programmed to believe we can attain physical fitness with a little effort, even though one visit to a Wal-Mart offers proof that the majority of us are not making that effort.) If you ask a couple of follow-up questions, you generally hear about Uncle Bob or Aunt Sue who lived the last x years of life locked in the Alzheimer's ward and over time recognized fewer and fewer loved ones. I share these concerns even though senility has not been a common trait in my family (yet). My anxiety over the issue of mental anxiety led me to expand my research into dementia and Alzheimer's. What I learned was a bit of a surprise.

Over and over, studies show that many of the best practices for promoting mental stability are similar to those that contribute to overall happiness or well-being in later life: a close-knit group of family and friends, a healthy lifestyle, a positive attitude, laughter, purpose. After a while, I was led to wonder if we could develop a list or matrix of what we should be looking for in the next leg of life's journey. If that were possible, we could then attempt to measure the various options for post-retirement activities against that backdrop and try to gauge the odds that we could achieve the desired outcomes of happiness and good mental health. Seemed to make sense on paper, anyway.

At some point in this process, it became apparent where I was headed. Could I take my list of possible passions and run them through the matrix? Would such an effort produce unwanted results? Any results? How do my strengths and weaknesses fit in? How do interesting distractions fit in? How does the spiritual and the desire to give back fit in? Then, it struck me: What if I could take the principles I had discovered in this process—the scale—and apply it to several possible passions and attempt to come to a somewhat objective assessment of their merits. In addition, the elements of the analysis should be pretty generic. Perhaps this process would be of benefit to others. To return to Otter's advice from *Animal House*, could I facilitate the ultimate road trip, and provide suitable checklists of things to pack and how otherwise to plan for the trip, all the while taking an enjoyable and exhilarating trip myself?

Is this a self-help book? I suppose it is, but it is not intended in the vein that I know all of the answers. First and foremost, I am not trained in any of the disciplines that seem to bear on these subjects. I barely survived Psychology 101 in college. I majored in accounting, for God's sake. And then law school. And then banking. And then mortgages. As the TV ads all proclaim, you should consult your doctor (and maybe your lawyer and your marriage counselor) before you take any advice I may give.

Also, let's be clear—there are no slam dunks, no sure bets. I don't think there are right answers (beyond, perhaps, your spiritual beliefs), but there are probabilities. For instance, if you take certain steps, you are more likely to live longer or be less likely to contract Alzheimer's, but there are no guarantees, no silver bullets—just better odds. My hope in this process has been to gain information and a way of thinking that helps me make better decisions. If that casts me in the self-help genre, so be it. I sincerely hope we both can help ourselves.

One complaint I have heard of some of the other books on this and related subjects is that the authors enjoy enough wherewithal to be able to a) retire in the first place; and b) pick any pastime they wish to enjoy. While statistics show that Americans are generally sticking with their paying jobs longer these days, the general principles described in the following pages apply irrespective of your current age or career stage. We all share the hope that at some point we will pass from fulfilling day-to-day responsibilities (e.g., raising and educating children, saving for retirement, caring for parents) and pass into an extended period of the pursuit of wanna-dos, instead of have-to-dos.

As for concerns about financial suitability, I get it. The sample of activities that I cover in the latter chapters were chosen, in part, with limited budgets in mind. One needn't be wealthy to play duplicate bridge or to join a Sacred Harp singing group. More to the point, I chose these pastimes as samples, as interesting and offbeat examples of paths that could be followed. The opportunities, and the level of financial commitment required, are endless.

A more prevalent, if often unstated, attitude is that taking on these issues is not worth the effort. When verbalized, this school of thought takes many forms: "Too much planning will deprive me of the spontaneity I need to enjoy retirement." "I know 'happy' when I feel it, and more focus on the topic is a waste of time." "I just plan to keep working and the rest will just take care of itself." "That is my wife's/husband's department." "I've got a whole stack of books waiting on me to retire." It is up to you to decide if you are ready for this trip and how you want to prep for it.

In the final analysis, this area is similar to the rest of life. As Yogi Berra so aptly put it: "If you don't know where you are going, you might not get there."

I can also provide you with some mnemonic tricks to use.

> *An elderly couple had dinner at another couple's house, and after eating, the wives left the table and went into the kitchen. The two gentlemen were talking, and one said, "Last night, we went to a new restaurant and it was really great. I would recommend it very highly."*
>
> *The other man inquired, "What's the name of the restaurant?"*
>
> *The first man thought and thought and finally said, "What is the name of that flower you give to someone you love? You know... the one that's red and has thorns?"*
>
> *"Do you mean a rose?"*
>
> *"Yes, that's the one," replied the man. He then turned toward the kitchen and yelled, "Rose, what was the name of that restaurant we went to last night?"*

Part I

Establishing the Rules

Do We Really Need a New Set of Rules?

1

Why Are You Reading This?

If you have made it this far (assuming you didn't skip the preface), I will take the liberty of making a few presumptions. First, I suspect that you are at least a Gen Xer, but more likely a Boomer. You likely were born in the Fifties or Sixties and have reached an age in life where you are thinking more and more about the next stage. Congratulations! You're aboveground and not gaga.

Perhaps you already have set a date for retirement, started scaling back your work hours, or gone ahead and taken the plunge. In any event, if you are under the age of 50 (unless you are helping others of more advanced ages), this book is probably a little premature for you. You might want to consider *You are a Badass: How to Stop Doubting Your Greatness and Start Living an Awesome Life*.[1] For those readers who have already been a badass for decades and need to move from awesome to happy, you've come to the right place.

It seems safe to assume that you are reasonably well-educated and thoughtful (in the sense of thinking about issues, not in the sense of being considerate, although you may qualify in both categories). After all, you are reading this book rather than watching reruns of *Real Housewives of Texarkana*. Given your intellect, you are willing, dare I say anxious, to pursue a studied approach to addressing issues that are likely to arise in the future. No whistling past the graveyard for you. You want to face facts and address pending life issues in an intellectually honest and forthright way.

That's how I wound up in this place. I had been lulled into a common misconception about retirement. I had been trained by the ads on TV during the football games to think that all it takes to retire successfully is to invest with the right brokerage house during my working years. Don't get me wrong—saving enough cabbage to live comfortably after your career is no easy task (just listen to all your friends who moan that they can't afford to retire), but having the finances needed for retirement is just the beginning.

The experts say that to achieve and maintain well-being in retirement, we all need to plan for this period well in advance. Planning for this stage of life should include not only having economic stability and a sufficiently sizeable nest egg but also a collection of other factors, such as quality of life, physical and mental health, education for life, cognitive stimuli, family and social relationships, personal and social well-being, and the prospects for new beginnings.[2] Oh, boy, did I have work to do…Given that you are spending some of your spare time thinking about non-financial matters and lifestyle choices, you are probably beyond the "how will I afford to retire" issue. You may not be in the 1%, but you are reasonably well-fixed from a financial security standpoint. As with most of us, you may not be completely content with the pile of gold that you have amassed for your golden years, but you are at least at a point where you are looking beyond the "do I have enough" question to "how will I spend it." It's a good thing, because I won't be addressing any financial management issues here, other than to be mindful of not coming up with any suggested courses of action that would require one to be wealthier than you to qualify. If you are looking for financial advice, go talk to one of those financial planners standing in line outside your door.

You very well may have a Type A personality or, at least, consider yourself to be a planner and a doer. You like to think of yourself as someone who can gather the facts, consider them objectively, chart a course of action based on what you learn, and—this is the important part—undertake the plan that you come up with. This personality characteristic probably explains how you managed to get your education, your career, and the assets that will allow you to retire. It also explains why you are working through the challenges you see coming down the pike. I'm just warning you, though: Your Type A-ness does not bode well for some of the advice I cover later about learning to chill out and let go of issues that threaten your mental well-being. Just warning you. I should know—this is one of my biggest continuing challenges.

I'm also going to assume that you've got a sense of humor. Here's a test: A woman gets on a bus with a baby. The bus driver says: "That's the ugliest baby I've ever seen. Ugh!" The woman goes to the rear of the bus and sits down, fuming. She says to the man next to her: "The driver just insulted me." The man says: "You go right up there and tell him off—go ahead. I'll hold your monkey for you." If you laughed out loud (or at least grinned) or said, "I've heard that one before and it's good," you have passed and may proceed.

If you saw no humor in it whatsoever, you flunked and should go read something else. You are going to be miserable reading this book. If you didn't find humor in the joke that was officially selected as the funniest joke in the United Kingdom in 2011[3], you are unlikely to enjoy any of my humor and you should go ahead and put yourself out of your reading misery. But just know before you leave, a good belly laugh now and again would make life a whole lot better (and likely longer) in the years ahead. If you don't like my jokes, you better find someone or something that makes you chuckle.

It wouldn't surprise me if you've had recent exposure to someone, probably a loved one, who didn't age well. Maybe Alzheimer's, maybe abject loneliness, leading to anger and bitterness. Maybe simply an extremely sedate and meaningless slide into the nursing home. Having witnessed some such unpleasantness may have led to discussions with a spouse or close friend about your desire to "make sure I don't end up that way." You may even have had a "put a pillow over my head before I get in that shape" conversation after seeing some extreme version of prolonged misery in a loved one's life. My hat's off to you, because you have moved beyond hoping to avoid an undesirable result to taking affirmative steps to address the risk.

So, what do you want out of the next few laps around the sun? How do you describe to yourself what is desirable for the next, and maybe last, part of your biography, and will it be an autobiography or will you just take what comes along? Have you given the same amount of thought to the question of how best to occupy your time post-career that you did to picking a career?

Whether they are heading for retirement or already there, most people would tell you (sometimes with a little prodding to get them to be honest and ask themselves the hard questions) that their No. 1 hope for the golden years is happiness.

At this stage, most of us have given up on eternal youth and have set our sights on the one thing that youth seemed to promise—joy. For years now, most of us have engaged in a form of delayed gratification. If we were lucky, we had jobs that were bearable, maybe even enjoyable (at least some of the time). For a fortunate few, work hasn't been work at all—it's been a blast the whole time.

But the vast majority of us have viewed work as, well, work. Enjoyable or not, it is something we have engaged in to allow us to meet our needs, whether they be financial or psychological, or both. But all along we have hoped and expected that one day we could reach a stage of less demanding responsibilities and more happiness. If nothing else, we could finally tackle that shelf of interesting books (including, perhaps, this one) that we never seemed to have time to read before. We have been looking forward to the next stage for a long, long time.

Wait, hold on a second. Are you sure that is the approach you want to take? Do you really think that merely going from a demanding career to a non-demanding lifestyle is the key to happiness? Research suggests otherwise. Moreover, research suggests that you are well served to think about these issues, preferably sooner rather than later. It would be nice to know the temperature of the water before taking the plunge in the pool.

For one thing, you need to stop and think about the very concept of "happiness." Does happiness equate to "joy" as suggested above, or is it better described by "well-being"? Does "fulfillment" play a role? Is this goal something different from just trying to extend your sell-by date? These are the types of questions I will explore in the next chapter, before we consider how to achieve the desired state. It is always nice to know what the goal is before embarking on the task.

It's time well spent to go through this thought process. According to the Social Security Administration, if you're a woman and you've managed to live to the age—what used to be considered the "ripe old age"—of 60, you can expect to live to 86.[4] Men who have made it to 60, on average, will make it to over 83. The longevity rate in the United States actually took a slight dip in 2015 but has generally been on a fairly steady march upward for as about as long as we've been a country.[5] One of the by-products of living longer, healthier lives is that retirement is being pushed off. According to *SmartAsset Magazine*, while average retirement ages vary from state to state, Americans typically plan to retire fully at age 63.[6] But all too often, professionals set their sights on the age at which they want to wrap up and how to afford it without much thought given to what comes next, even though "next" will, in all likelihood, last a long time. Have you been so busy getting to the career finish line that you haven't thought about the next race and what you are going to do during the last third of your life to really enjoy it?

It is also important to realize that our bodies may have other plans for us. If we equate happiness with sitting in front of a TV alone, drinking beer, eating potato chips, and binge-watching old episodes of *Bewitched*, there is a good chance that our happy period will be short-lived. Our bodies will quickly begin to decay into dotage, and our minds will start to wander into senility.

I don't want to sound like your mother here, but a key component of achieving sustainable happiness is making appropriate lifestyle choices. Without question, one very important lifestyle choice involves the physical—exercise. This book is not focused on exercise, but that is not because I don't think it is important. All studies show that good, regular exercise, particularly as you grow older, is a key to enjoying life as you hit your sixties and beyond. To best accomplish this, there are many books and many suggested regimens. In fact, there likely is a fitness center within walking distance of your home and an attractive young trainer in spandex yoga pants waiting for you. I will spend a few pages discussing exercise, but primarily how it intersects with an active lifestyle. It is, however, the engaged and challenging lifestyle, rather than stomach crunches, that will be the focus of most of this book.

Now, I also don't want this to sound like a Geritol ad. As far as I can tell, there are no magic elixirs that guarantee optimal enjoyment during a phase of life that is packed with physical and mental challenges. There are, however, steps you can take and ways of thinking that will improve the odds of leading a happier life for a longer period. If nothing else, I have found benefit in stepping back and just giving some thought to what lies ahead and what my plan of attack ought to be.

Don't be daunted by thoughts that your personality is not amenable to change. The studies seem to show that to a greater or lesser extent, you can teach an old dog new tricks. Even an old dog like you. Even an old dog without a sense of humor can learn to cackle a bit, but it's all about attitude. You gotta wanna. I encourage you to approach the topics that I cover over the rest of Part I with an "open mind and a willing heart." Whether or not you choose to apply these concepts to some real life adventures, as I do in Part II, is up to you.

Whether or not you continue reading what I have to say on these subjects, you deserve a pat on the back for thinking about this stuff. It is always easier to tell yourself that you'll have time to think about the future sometime in the future. But in the back of your mind, you know. You know that there is no better time than right now. Listen to your Type A personality one more time, and try to come up with a plan for the best part of your life.

Let's start by looking at what the term "happiness" really means.

But, first, a story about the importance of rules.

> *Two great white sharks swimming in the ocean spy some surfers. The younger one licks his lips and makes a beeline for them.*
>
> *"Just a minute," says his father, stopping him. "First we swim around them with just the tip of our fins showing."*
>
> *And they do.*
>
> *"Now we swim around them a few times with all our fins showing."*
>
> *And they do.*
>
> *"Now we eat everybody."*
>
> *When they have both eaten all they can, the son asks, "Dad, why didn't we just eat them when we first saw them?"*
>
> *"Because they taste better without all the poop inside."*

2

Just Do What Makes You Happy

I hate to write. In high school, I took procrastination to a new level when the annual term paper was due, always waiting to the last minute before forcing myself to put pen to paper. I managed to make it through college with a business administration degree and without taking a single English course. Courses in other disciplines that required term papers were a source of months of dread, followed by sleepless stretches of frenzied research and writing.

Then I got to law school, where a course in legal writing was mandatory the first semester. Second year brought a spot on the law review, a student-run legal journal that required intense writing responsibilities and strident, and in some cases, petty, editorial review of all content. Third year—an editorial board position and more writing.

In my last year of law school, I was able to land a job after graduation as a law clerk to a judge on the federal court of appeals based in New Orleans. The duties for that post involved intense periods of writing memos for the judge to help prepare him for cases he was to hear and then drafts of the opinions once the judges had decided which way to go on the case. The writing responsibilities were interspersed with stints of research in the courthouse library. (Online research tools were just in their infancy at the time.)

After my year in New Orleans, I was fortunate enough to spend a year in Washington, D.C., clerking for Justice Lewis F. Powell on the U.S. Supreme Court for the term that began the first Monday in October of 1983. To date, that job entailed the most challenging work-year of my life, in large part because all I did was write.

Essentially, a clerk writes from before breakfast in the morning until well into the evening six days a week for a year. There is very little research, because the lawyers for each side of the case brief all of the issues and there are research assistants assigned the task of ferreting out any additional materials you may need. Your job as a clerk is to read and digest the materials, ascertain the relevant legal principles, apply those principles to the facts of individual cases, and commit the Court's conclusions regarding the application of the law to the facts to writing. And there are many, many cases. But I survived and have a volume of written work to prove that I could put thoughts on paper in some logical order.

Over my ensuing career, writing has continued to play an important role. That role has, without question, evolved as my career has mutated, from research memos and legal documents as a young lawyer, to business letters and speeches as a businessman and government employee, to congressional testimony and op-eds later in life. Along the way, I have also written the occasional article, such as a tribute to Justice Powell following his death for my old school's law review. In short, writing has been a constant, and it is still excruciating.

So what does this autobiographical sequence have to do with happiness? What I have found over the years is that writing, while a form of discomfort and drudgery, is also a source of intense personal satisfaction. Whether it is hitting "send" on an e-mail to a client or presenting a dry and detailed paper on mortgage regulation reform, completion of a writing task provides a sense of accomplishment. And I am constantly surprised that something I feared at an early age, loathed during my formative years, and still dread as I approach each new challenge can also result in a form of pleasure after it is completed.

Other people may not share these feelings about writing, neither the dread it engenders nor the sense of accomplishment upon completion. It is, however, the best way for me to describe the difference between feeling good on a short-term basis and enjoying long-term well-being at a very personal level. I suffer from what seems to be a fairly common ailment among writers—procrastination. When I have a writing task in front of me, virtually any other project seems to be more appealing. Once I finally sit down at the keyboard, however, I lose track of time and genuinely enjoy organizing my thoughts and converting them to the written word. When the product is complete, it provides self-satisfaction, and the longer the project, the greater the level of satisfaction.

My experience with writing is not unique. My wife is an artist and achieves the same level of contentment from painting. Moreover, she loses track of time when she is in her studio, and she is in a better mood when she emerges. She suffers, however, from the same illogical bouts of procrastination as I do about writing assignments while she awaits the arrival of her creative muse. Once she gets herself to the studio, she enjoys it so much that she finds it hard to leave.

It turns out that the sense of well-being I achieve from writing and my wife gets from painting is a circumstance that has caught the attention of thoughtful observers for millennia. Had I been listening in high school that week in world history class that Mr. Maher talked about ancient Greece, or if I had taken Western Civilization or philosophy in college, I might have learned something that would have been much more life-altering than the date of the Battle of Thermopylae.

Thinkers of that day and age began to distinguish between the type of happiness that results from a sense of accomplishment as I have described writing and painting for Mr. and Mrs. Couch and the type of momentary happiness that occurs from quenching a thirst or riding a roller coaster. The ancient Greeks employed different terms to describe these human conditions: eudaemonia and hedone.

Almost 2,400 years ago, Aristotle spent a lot of time thinking about these concepts and putting his thoughts down on paper, or whatever it was you wrote on in those days. In his *Nicomachean Ethics*[7], he reasoned that our quest for happiness is somewhat unique because, unlike virtually everything else that we do, happiness is an end in itself. Deep down, all of our other activities—earning a living, courting a companion, attempting to shoot even-par, throwing a $20 bill in the offering plate at church—are directed at one level or another at the goal of producing happiness. Happiness itself, by contrast, is not a means to any other end. Even trying to make someone else happy is a way of heading to our own happy place.

Where Aristotle would diverge from society's current view of happiness is in defining what constitutes happiness. Most of us tend to equate happiness with momentary pleasure or temporary joy. The first lick of the ice-cream cone on a hot afternoon. Hitting the jackpot on the slot machine. Opening gifts at the birthday party. Aristotle would refer to these feelings as hedone, which is the precursor to the English word "hedonism." This self-indulgence is not the type of happiness that he would encourage us to pursue.

Instead, he would focus on another Greek word for happiness—eudaemonia. In Aristotle's view, happiness is not to be measured by what you feel at the moment, but rather by the ultimate value of your life as measured by how well you have lived up to your full potential as a human being. Hedonic happiness is all about having fun and satisfying various appetites, whether they be hunger, boredom, or a craving for drugs or sex. Eudaemonic happiness, by contrast, involves long-term focus on a variety of elements, including health, wealth, knowledge, reasoning, and friends, to strive for excellence in worthwhile pursuits and enrichment of life. In short, a virtuous life is a happy life. Or stated another way, it's not all about being the life of the toga party.

But thinking about happiness didn't stop when ancient Greece hit the wall of history. Similar themes were stressed later by St. Augustine and St. Thomas Aquinas. There are also parallels between Aristotle's goal of eudaemonia and the "Middle Path" in Buddhism. The great Islamic philosopher Abu Hamid al-Ghazali focused on a similar theme around 1100 A.D. in his seminal work, *The Alchemy of Happiness*, when he opined: "He who knows himself is truly happy."[8] Scores of other thinkers through the centuries have contemplated the best approach to finding true happiness. In some cases the thought leaders built upon Aristotle's work. In others, they didn't know Greece or Aristotle ever graced the Earth, but they nevertheless arrived at similar conclusions through completely independent thought processes. Tends to make you think they might have been on to something, huh?

What does modern research say on the subject? Since the 1960s, academicians from a wide variety of disciplines have ramped up the study of happiness, including experts in the fields of psychology, gerontology, general medicine, and economics. Despite efforts by researchers around the globe and seemingly universal interest, happiness continues to be a fuzzy and fluid concept. How you define it, promote it, and measure it often depends on the angle from which you approach it. For instance, many religious writers focus on the contentment of the adherents to their beliefs. A host of purveyors of other types of spirits promise happiness without spirituality, from single-malt Scotch to herbal teas. The modern roads to happiness seem to be endless. Scientific consensus, however, seems to be jelling around concepts that would sound familiar to old Mr. Aristotle.

First, there does seem to be widespread agreement that a significant portion of our level of happiness is totally out of our hands. That is because roughly 50% of our happiness meter is hard-wired in our genetic code. Nevertheless, another significant portion (some studies suggest about 40%) is subject to our self-control, with the remainder (give or take 10%) determined by life circumstances, such as the part of town we are born in and whether we have good parents. However you look at it, a large chunk of our level of satisfaction with our lives is self-determined. Stated another way—if I wanna be happy, it's up to me to make it happen.

In the early 1980s, a body of scientific work emerged that built upon the concepts of eudaemonia similar to those espoused by Aristotle in the fourth century BC. A seminal work published by psychologist Carol Ryff made the case that psychological well-being (as a stand-in for Aristotle's eudaemonia) is the key to life satisfaction and good mental health.[9] The concept has been wrapped up in the much broader field of "positive psychology," a term coined by Abraham Maslow in the early 1950s.[10] In layman's terms, proponents of positive psychology focus on what is right in a person's psyche and making it better rather than focusing on those who have gone off their mental tracks and trying to fix them.

As developed over the past 25-plus years by Dr. Ryff and other researchers, the scientific literature has explored the concept of well-being in a variety of life situations. The proponents of positive psychology focus on a few key factors in the way we conduct our lives with the hope of achieving a prolonged state of upbeat outlooks on our own conditions. Those conditions then correlate with feelings of contentment or well-being.

In her early work, a system of six key determinants of well-being emerged from Dr. Ryff's work. According to her research the following six factors are the bellwethers of happiness:

1. Purpose—the extent to which you feel your life has meaning and direction
2. Autonomy—whether you view yourself as living in accord with your own convictions

3. Personal growth—the extent to which you are making use of your personal talents and potential
4. Environmental control—how well you are mastering your life situations
5. Positive relationships—the depth of your ties with your significant others
6. Self-acceptance—the level of your own self-awareness, self-forgiveness, and self-acceptance. [11]

As it turns out, we are not just talking about contentment here. While walking around with a smile on your face may seem like a worthy goal in and of itself, the side effects of such a lifestyle go well beyond personal satisfaction. A body of evidence is building that a focus on these elements and the conscious pursuit of well-being have the additional salutary benefits of reducing risk of disease and leading to a longer life.

At this point you may be thinking: "Gimme a break! I've heard all of this kind of BS before when I fell asleep watching the 10 o'clock news and woke up to that paid TV advertisement about some powder I put in a blender and my whole life will change." I confess that I had the same sort of reaction at first. Let's face it—I'm a lawyer with an accounting background, about as far from psychologist as you can get. But as I dug more and more into it I became more and more convinced that this is the real stuff—the key (or really keys) to contentment.

In a nutshell, it comes down to this: By working toward a happy (as in eudaemonic happy) life, my remaining time on earth is more likely to be longer, healthier, and more contented. Thus, it seems like a worthwhile pursuit to look at each of Dr. Ryff's six slices of the "happy-meal pie" in a little more detail, and apply them to my own personality and current situation.

1. Purpose in Life

Given that my starting point for this discussion is that I, like most of my readers, am approaching one of life's flexion points, this factor is particularly relevant. For the past 30 or so years, I have been pursuing a career that has (roughly) followed the same path. After achieving some measure of education, I got a job utilizing that education. Some might look at my paying jobs over that career and argue that I meandered, from accounting to law to banking to mortgage banking to government and back to law. I would argue that closer examination would reveal more direction generally through the financial services industry. Irrespective of the description of the past, what I am contemplating for the future entails potentially significant changes.

Of particular relevance for this discussion is the vortex of disparate objectives swirling through my thoughts as I contemplate retirement: less structure, more socially meaningful outcomes, fewer rules, more autonomy, less responsibility, more downtime, less stress, more recreation time, fewer neckties, more family time. Somehow, more purpose isn't high on the list.

Then a dose of reality wafts over my thoughts: I have devoted so much time to work over the last 35 years that I haven't developed any real hobbies. My kids are out of the nest, and my spouse has her own life as do my close friends who have stuck with me during my years of career focus. My Type A personality may have served me well during the last life phase, but it doesn't play well with a low-key, kicked-back approach. While I'm on the subject, how does one do "low-key, kick-back"? Does any of this soul-searching sound familiar?

My guess is that these types of concerns are shared by many who are thinking about retirement. Over the past couple of years, I have made a point of asking all recent retirees with whom I come in contact: "What are you doing with all of your time these days?" In the vast majority of cases, the answer comes back that, despite their pre-retirement fears, they have no trouble filling up their days. The old rule that the job will fill up the time allotted seems to apply with vengeance now that they have no paid employment. Personal chores that used to take a couple of hours on the weekends now occupy days. New, must-see TV programs occupy most evenings (and some afternoons and mornings). The weekly golf game has turned into thrice-a-week leisurely golf outings.

Unfortunately, this carefree existence doesn't really comport with the psychologists' idea of life purpose. Even at this new stage of life, purpose requires goals. It is those goals that lead to direction. It is those goals and conduct of your life in the direction of those goals that provide meaning. And the combination of those goals, direction, and meaning that will make getting out of bed enjoyable for the coming decades.

2. Autonomy

In Dr. Ryff's way of thinking, truly autonomous people are independent and they attempt to regulate their own behavior from within themselves. As such, they are able to resist social pressures to think and act in certain ways, evaluating themselves by their own personal standards. An autonomous person is not really all that concerned about the expectations and evaluations of others, relying more on personal benchmarks to judge personal behaviors.

I would like to think that, almost by definition, the process I am undertaking here is an exercise in autonomy, starting with the self-examination I undertook in the early stages of this project. By writing down on a piece of paper my own personal SWOT analysis of my strengths, weaknesses, opportunities, and threats, I hoped to set parameters for the decisions that needed to follow. In my mind, provided I was brutally honest with myself, I could chart a course independent of the expectations of others. If that course proves successful, I can take the credit; if not, there is no one else to blame. (I will admit that I asked my wife to take a look at the results of the SWOT as a check on self-delusion. Either I hit the mark or she was too kind to point out any material errors. She did help me make some refinements.)

I also feel comfortable that I am not buffeted by social pressures to act in a particular way. I have always prided myself on being an independent thinker and not subject to herd mentality. This issue is probably one that is, however, difficult to self-judge. We are all creatures of our cultures, and our thoughts are inexorably influenced by our surroundings. To that end, while I honestly believe that I am somewhat immune to social pressures, there is no doubt that I am carried along in those currents and my periodic efforts to swim up or across social streams are modest in the long-term flow of things. Nevertheless, all in all, I give myself high marks on the autonomy front.

3. Personal Growth

An important element in Carol Ryff's formula for well-being is a commitment to continual personal growth and development. In her view, happy people are open to new experiences, with an ongoing sense of striving to realize their own potential. For these folks, a willingness to make life changes driven by awareness of personal strengths generally leads to improvements in life conditions and personal behaviors over time.

In a sense, this is one area where a successful career may work against you. As you succeed in your area of expertise, there is a tendency to get complacent and comfortable in your niche—you may get stuck in the rut that your success has dug for you. In addition, you are so successful that it is difficult to find the time to get out of it. You also get tired. It is harder and harder to get out of your comfort zone and try new stuff. Such complacency can compound itself if you retire and go from unbridled devotion to your career to post-retirement life without external interests to develop. This is a problem, as the science of positive psychology has put fancy names on one of my favorite sayings: You rest, you rust, you rot.

Now, I have stumbled on one of my personal dilemmas. I struggle with walking away from a job that is a culmination of many years of developing skill sets, a reputation, and a wonderful professional network. What idiot, in reasonably good health, would voluntarily turn his back on the opportunity to finish playing out the career that has been so many years in the making.

In some ways, my meandering job history provides me an advantage here. Having bounced from the law to commercial banking to mortgage banking to government service and back to the law, I have had the opportunity to see my field from a variety of perspectives. (One of my closest friends says I just can't keep a job.) The problem is that each of my positions seems to have been all consuming, or, at least, I allowed each to consume the vast majority of my time and attention. It's all I know. As a result, I now find that I am somewhat a prisoner of my success and I don't have a convenient and challenging outlet to retire into.

4. Environmental Control

Dr. Ryff's elements of well-being include the concept that people who have a sense of mastery and competence in managing their external environments will enjoy life more. By effectively choosing opportunities or creating situations suitable to their personal needs and values, such people are more satisfied with the management of their everyday affairs. It stands to reason that going to the effort of proactively working toward your personal goals and believing that you're in control of that process will make you happier about your situation.

In fact, this process of taking ownership of the final stage of my life is precisely the point of the whole exercise. But "mastery and competence" are pretty high standards that suggest a level of control that goes well beyond asking questions and doing some reading. Am I fooling myself by inflating, in my own mind, the magnitude of the effect I can have? Perhaps, but I take some comfort in the knowledge that I am working through these issues and developing a plan. I have gained satisfaction that I am at least trying to address the challenges and coming up with a plan to deal with them. In fact, the biggest frustration that I have is that my day job keeps me from devoting the amount of time I would like to properly prepare for ditching my day job. On this factor, I am comfortable that my search for answers indicates the type of environmental management that contributes to well-being.

5. Positive Relationships

One of the areas particularly stressed by Dr. Ryff in maintaining well-being is having warm, satisfying, and trusting relationships with others. Her research has found that happy people generally are concerned about the welfare of others, and capable of strong empathy, affection, and intimacy. Effective managers of personal networks understand the give-and-take of human relationships.

I am pretty satisfied with this element of my life. One of the benefits of a career that has spanned law firms, businesses, government, and a variety of volunteer community service roles has been the development of a wide circle of friends and acquaintances. More importantly, I have a smaller but still relatively large group of close friends of many years with whom I have trusting relationships.

The challenge for me is not to take the network for granted. My boss when I first got into banking almost 30 years ago, John Oliver, had an insightful saying that I have tried to take to heart: "Friends come and go, but enemies tend to accumulate." The first half of John's adage is the part that requires more work than I would like to think. One of the brutal truths of my professional life is that work and travel schedules take an awful toll on my personal relationships. Many times after a long week on the road, the last thing I want to do is seek out other people and reconnect. One of the benefits of this process, however, has been to make me realize how important those relationships are and how much my long-term well-being depends on my investment of time and effort in maintaining them. That network of close friends is so important I devote an entire chapter to it later.

The second half of John's saying also poses a challenge for me. The mix of Type A personality, a lack of patience, and my mother's temper can combine to ruffle feathers. I recognize that my desire to achieve results has from time to time led to conflict, and that conflict is not a good way to build positive relationships. In fact, it sounds much more like a formula that leads to road rage. But at least I am aware of this volatile mixture of ingredients, and somewhat optimistic that I have made some progress in disarming my internal IEDs as I move toward retirement. Unfortunately, making amends for past transgressions is much harder. As John would say, enemies tend to accumulate.

6. Self-acceptance

In Dr. Ryff's view, truly happy people possess a positive attitude toward themselves. Such people are realistic about their personalities, acknowledging, even accepting, the many facets of those personalities—both good and bad. Moreover, such people are able to get beyond the mistakes they may have made in the past and generally feel positive about their past lives.

Once again the SWOT analysis comes into play. One key to this self-analysis, especially as it applies to this factor, is the need for brutal self-honesty. Suffice it to say that in my frank self-assessment, I identified plenty of traits that need improvement as well as a number of risk factors, not to mention a host of instances in my past life that I would do differently if given the opportunity. And I have to assume that, even with my attempt to be up-front with myself, my ego probably sanded some of the rougher edges of my personality. Nevertheless, I suppose I get pretty high marks for at least trying to catalog my attributes and shortcomings. Where I fall short is in the area of getting past the past.

When I conducted my close look in the personality mirror, it caused me to dredge several episodes in the past of which I am not proud. Many of those resulted in violation of the second part of the John Oliver rule—the accumulation of enemies. I also have come to realize that I am bad to carry a grudge. Grudges do not comport with well-being in Carol Ryff's worldview. But if self-awareness is a big part of the battle, at least I have engaged the enemy. On the list of items to work on, cutting myself more slack on past mistakes goes right next to working on changing those personality traits that cause friction with others. My goal here is to focus on future improvements and not dwell on the past.

Over the last three decades, Dr. Ryff has continued to massage the framework she first laid out in the 1980s. In addition, her basic concepts have been adopted and extended by hosts of other psychologists. One of her disciples is noted psychologist Martin Seligman, the Director of the Positive Psychology Center at the University of Pennsylvania. Dr. Seligman further refined Ryff's elements of a happy life into three broad categories: the Pleasant Life, the Good Life, and the Meaningful Life.[12] The Pleasant Life, which sounds a lot like Aristotle's version of hedonism, is about positive, usually fleeting, emotions. He cites examples such as the pleasure that can be obtained through drugs, shopping, masturbation, and television. He pretty well covers the waterfront, I'd say. The only thing he leaves out is chocolate.

True happiness, in his view, goes farther than this and encompasses the Good Life and the Meaningful Life. The Good Life, in contrast to the Pleasant Life, is about identifying one's strengths and virtues and using them as frequently as possible in work, love, play, and retirement to produce "abundant and authentic" gratification. But Seligman doesn't stop with achieving the Good Life. There is another achievable level of happiness, the Meaningful Life, which adds one further ingredient: identifying and using one's highest strengths in order to belong to or to serve something larger than you are.

Seligman summarizes his approach to happiness with the acronym PERMA.[13]

Under PERMA, we are happiest when we have:
1. Positive emotions (optimism, good food, good times, etc.)
2. Engagement (the absorption of a challenging reality)
3. Relationships (special, social ties)
4. Meaning (a perceived quest to belong to something greater than ourselves)
5. Accomplishments (realizing tangible goals)

Clearly, there are lots of overlaps between Seligman's PERMA and the Ryff well-being factors. In my view, an important addition to Ryff's work in Seligman's thinking is the addition of the first element: positive emotions. At one level, I understand the concept of eudaemonia, but it gets pretty touchy-feely pretty quickly. The concepts of self-acceptance, autonomy, and meaning begin to conjure up images of Haight-Ashbury mind expansion and Far Eastern spiritualism. It's kind of nice, therefore, for a highly regarded psychologist to proclaim that there is a role for good old-fashioned fun and comfort food. Now *that* is a self-help bandwagon I can crawl aboard.

Once having consumed the caramel-covered donut in pursuit of "positive emotion," however, the introduction of this concept does raise a host of questions in my mind. Is all fun good for me? What if I use chemicals (including bourbon, pot, and Kools) to induce that state? Can I have too much of a good thing? What if it is fun at someone else's expense (a straight man, the butt of a joke)? Where's the line between fun and excitement? Am I overthinking this? No question that you have to be careful not to stop at the "P" in "PERMA," but it's nice to have it as part of the equation.

The rest of Dr. Seligman's formula fits comfortably into Ryff's six factors, with one overlay—the concept of doing something meaningful with your efforts. In his view, maximum happiness is achieved once your efforts result in a benefit to others. Barbara Bradley Hagerty refers to this extra element as "generativity."[14] Whatever you call it, I equate it with the warm feeling that comes along with doing something good for someone else. To me, it borders on—no, it actually lands smack in the middle of—spirituality, and is a highly personal element. Personal, but important, and each of us can achieve the Meaningful Life only after first deciding subjectively what is worthwhile.

Some observers will be quick to draw parallels between the Meaningful Life and various established religious doctrines. I address this in a separate (short) chapter on spirituality, but I am mindful that religion is one of the three deadly topics to avoid at a dinner party (along with sex and politics). My purpose here is not to proselytize for any one religion (or no religions) but to point out that the spiritual component is important. Now, get on your knees, or your prayer rug, or your yoga mat and get with your own spirituality.

Another refinement to the general principles laid out by Carol Ryff was provided by Mihaly Csikszentmihalyi. (Try saying that name three times, real fast—henceforth he will be known to us as Dr. C.) In his groundbreaking work in the 1990s, *Flow: The Psychology of Optimal Experience*, Dr. C proclaims: "The best moments in our lives are not the passive, receptive, relaxing times...The best moments usually occur if a person's body or mind is stretched to its limits in a voluntary effort to accomplish something difficult and worthwhile."[15] Dr. C's work builds on the groundbreaking work of Abraham Maslow in the 1940s entitled "A Theory of Human Motivation."[16] Maslow's work outlined a hierarchy of needs that are common to all of us, including safety, belonging, love, and self-esteem. At the top of his pyramid, Maslow eventually put "self-actualization" and "self-transcendence." Dr. C extended these concepts in his study of happiness. In his view, once someone gets to a place where they are fully occupied in an endeavor that uses their natural skills and talents to achieve a purpose, they have achieved an "optimal experience" and they lose all track of time and effort.

Dr. C describes this condition as being in "flow." Wikipedia, the font of all knowledge, provides this definition of "flow": "In positive psychology, flow, also known as the zone, is the mental state of operation in which a person performing an activity is fully immersed in a feeling of energized focus, full involvement, and enjoyment in the process of the activity."[17] For me, flow is viewing happiness or well-being through the lens of contentment—when you are lost in and fully enjoying what you are doing, you are truly content. Dr. C has a much more scientific analysis, explaining that human brains can only process so much information at any given time. If you are fully focused on an activity, your brain will shove aside more mundane issues like care and worry, making the experience seem more pleasant.[18]

Dr. C says that once we are in flow, we exercise control over the contents of our consciousness rather than allowing ourselves to be buffeted by the winds of our surroundings. Dr. C says that once in flow, "the experience is so enjoyable that people will continue to do it even at great cost, for the sheer sake of doing it." As someone trained in business and lawyering rather than psychology, I think the concept of finding happiness through flow is a close cousin to the goal of finding a job doing something that you love to do, so that you will never have to "work."

Whether we are seeking flow or the Good Life or well-being or just plain happiness, a host of questions immediately come to mind about the practical application of the principles set forth in all of these scholarly works. How do I go about changing my approach to everyday living to focus on Ryff's elements or Seligman's PERMA model? What if I don't buy into the "consciousness" stuff? Are some of the elements more important than others? Do I have to be optimistic about stuff, when experience tells me the worst is going to happen? Do I have to be a social animal, even though I really just like to curl up with a good book?

Many of these questions are addressed by a leading positive psychologist, Sonja Lyubomirsky, in *The How of Happiness*.[19] Dr. L reviews the results of the research of her peers, including Drs. Ryff and C, and concludes that focusing on happiness in one's life is a worthy goal, not just because it makes you feel better but also because it will boost "energy, creativity, and [your] immune system, foster better relationships, fuel higher productivity at work, and even lead to a longer life."[20] In her opinion, happiness is the Holy Grail.

From the outset, however, Dr. L cautions that we have a limited amount of room in which to maneuver our happiness ship. She refers to research (also accepted by Dr. Seligman and a broad swath of those in the field of positive psychology) that concludes that 50% of our "happiness set point" is attributable to our genetic makeup. Another 10% is determined by our circumstances, such as being raised in a good home, living in a crappy neighborhood, or suffering from a chronic illness. Add it up and that leaves only 40% of the happiness chips available for playing life's game.[21] Skipping ahead, one of Dr. L's happy techniques is optimism. In that vein, I'll restate the hypothesis: While our glass is 60% full already, we all are the masters of a huge chunk, 40%, of our happiness serving. It is up to us to fill the mug to the brim and start chugging.

Dr. L has compiled a list of 12 happiness activities. These are practical techniques that she suggests you incorporate into your daily activities to boost your happiness quotient. She admits from the outset that her list of activities seems over-the-top kitschy at first reading, but you just have to get over the sense that you are reading a Hallmark greeting card. Her suggested activities are:

1. Expressing gratitude
2. Cultivating optimism
3. Avoiding overthinking and social comparison
4. Practicing acts of kindness
5. Nurturing relationships
6. Developing strategies for coping
7. Learning to forgive
8. Doing more activities that truly engage
9. Savoring life's joys

10. Committing to goals
11. Practicing religion and spirituality
12. Taking care of your body[22]

In addition to admitting how corny some of these sound, Dr. L also recognizes that individual participants will find some of these steps more appealing (and doable) than others. To make the most of this reality, she advises focusing on the four activities that best fit the individual. She even offers a quiz to help determine the top four.[23]

Interestingly, Dr. L doesn't rank the activities in terms of impact on one's level of happiness. Her method, instead, presumes that an activity is more likely to have an impact if the individual's personality is suited to it. This assumption makes intuitive sense because you are more likely to stick with a course of action you enjoy, that matches your values, and that comes naturally to you. Is there a minimum number of activities to pursue? She recommends focusing on one to three initially, and ultimately think about trying to pay attention to all of them.

It doesn't take a genius to tie each of Dr. L's 12 activities to one of the letters in Doc Seligman's PERMA framework or to the slices in Dr. Ryff's well-being pie. Clearly, there is a pattern developing here. Dr. L does, however, help someone like me understand the everyday application of the principles. In Southern parlance, this is called getting the hay down to where the horses can get to it.

So, I took Dr. L's quiz and identified activities 8 (more engaging activities), 1 (expressing gratitude), 10 (goal commitment), and 2 (optimism cultivation) as the areas on which I should focus. (As a test of the test—or maybe a test of the test-taker—I asked my wife of 38 years to complete the questionnaire as if she were me. She ranked "Avoiding overthinking and social comparison" as the closest fit for me. I ranked it 10 out of 12. Hmmm...maybe I'm overthinking this.)

Doc Seligman has more recently taken his positive psychology program to a new level in a recent book, *Flourish*.[24] Under the *Flourish* model, Seligman maintains that to achieve maximum well-being, an individual (or an organization if you want to take the concept that far) must determine his/her character strengths and then apply them in the most meaningful way to achieve the greatest accomplishments. All of this makes perfect sense until you overlay human nature. Pretty soon, to many of us mere mortals, this begins to sound a lot more like work than happiness. Kind of like getting a Ph.D. in Happiness before you've graduated from Happiness High School.

Doc Seligman also has a test that you can self-administer to help you determine what your greatest character strengths are so you can use them on your path to "flourishment." In fact, Dr. Seligman opines at the outset that since 50% of your positive/negative switches are hard coded in our genes before you set out, you need to focus like a laser on those areas where you excel. When I take Dr. Seligman's test, I score highest on sense of humor, but self-discipline is nowhere in sight. Under the auspices of the University of Pennsylvania's Positive Psychology Center, you can take a variety of tests to help you self-identify those areas where you have a leg up on well-being and those areas that need work.[25]

I have to confess that Dr. Seligman's latest extension of the concepts of positive psychology in *Flourish* leave me somewhat flat. What if one of those preset switches is "doesn't take advice well"? In addition, the *Flourish* approach in my mind smacks of an HOV lane for overachievers. I have to wonder whether an individual who is naturally predisposed to planning, maximizing strengths, minimizing weaknesses, and postponing gratification really needs much help putting all the pieces together.

And then, there are the rest of us. We're not so sure about all this touchy-feely inward-looking stuff. For us, the most important element in Seligman's PERMA program is "positive emotion" and for us it is spelled F-U-N. We just want to have fun and we don't need some hoo-dad with a Ph.D. in psychology to tell us when we are having it. We know it when we do it. Right?

Actually, I have to believe (and hope) that there is a vast middle ground. We all know on a certain level that a life devoted to only hedonistic pursuits looks good in the magazines, but isn't truly desirable. For one thing, if all you do is drink Slippery Nipples by the pool all day, every day, eventually it's going to get old and you are going to get fat and wrinkly. There has to be more to life in retirement, even if we don't buy into the theory that you want to perfect your happiness score and become a Master Flourisher. It is my self-appointed task to determine what my sweet spot is and how to get there. Hopefully, you will find the process appealing and try the same thing.

All of this brings me back to where I started this chapter—I hate to write. But I have to admit that I get a huge charge out of putting the finishing touches on a writing project. At that point, I feel as if I have engaged fully and produced something. Call it pride, or self-satisfaction, or fulfillment, but is it happiness? One element of the flow and *Flourish* vein has application to my writing activities: While I have to force myself to sit down at the word-processor, I do lose track of time while I am writing. Perhaps, I have found well-being in the unlikeliest of places. Is there a method I can use to determine if writing is what I need to achieve Aristotle's concept of eudaemonia?

What about you? I'm not presuming that writing is necessarily in your flow bag, but do the precepts of positive psychology indicate that you are on the right track as you approach or deal with retirement? All of the work that has been done in this field, dating back to Aristotle, suggests that you would be well-served to think about your plans through the lens of improving your sense of well-being. But are there other considerations as well? Let's consider another relevant question: Are you playing with a full deck?

But one final reminder: Even if you do everything right, there are no guarantees.

> *A middle-aged woman had a heart attack and was taken to the hospital. While on the operating table, she had a near-death experience. Seeing God, she asked, "Is my time up?"*
>
> *God said, "No, you have another 43 years, two months, and eight days to live."*
>
> *Upon recovery, the woman decided to stay in the hospital and have a face-lift, lip enhancement, boob job, liposuction, and a tummy tuck. After her last operation, she was released from the hospital. While crossing the street on her way home, she was hit and killed by an ambulance. Arriving in front of God, she demanded, "I thought you said I had another 40-plus years? Why didn't you pull me out of the path of the ambulance?"*
>
> *God replied, "Gurl, I didn't even recognize you!"*

Also, our concept of happiness changes over time.

> *A guy is 71 years old and loves to fish. He was sitting in his boat the other day when he heard a voice say, "Pick me up."*
>
> *He looked around and couldn't see anyone. He thought he was dreaming when he heard the voice again say, "Pick me up." He looked in the water and there, floating on the top, was a frog.*
>
> *The man said, "Are you talking to me?" The frog said, "Yes, I'm talking to you. Pick me up. Then, kiss me and I'll turn into the most beautiful woman you have ever seen. I'll give you more sexual pleasure than you've ever imagined."*
>
> *The man looked at the frog for a short time, reached over, picked it up carefully, and placed it in his front breast pocket.*
>
> *Then the frog said, "What, are you nuts? Didn't you hear what I said? I said kiss me and we can have wonderful sex."*
>
> *He opened his pocket, looked at the frog, and said, "Nah, at my age I'd rather have a talking frog."*

3

I'm Driving Me Crazy

I've got some good news and some bad news. First, the good news: Due to a variety of factors, most of them having to do with advancements in health care, in our lifetime, lifetimes have gotten significantly longer. In the United States, once you reach the age of 60, odds are you won't expire until after you have celebrated your 84th birthday. If you are a woman, that birthday is 86. As a result of this increased life expectancy and the fact that the biggest wave of the Boomers in the Baby Boom are passing well into their 60s, in the year 2060, the number of Americans expected to be in our 90s will reach 98 million.[26]

Now, the bad news: The chances of contracting Alzheimer's disease or another form of dementia get higher as you age. Just by living longer, we are dramatically increasing the likelihood we will end up in that place many of us dread the most. The Alzheimer's Association projects that the number of people with dementia will triple by the year 2050.[27] In fact, odds today are that one in three people will live long enough to wind up materially mentally impaired. Look at the person on your left and the person on your right, and then realize that one of you is going nuts.

Also, if you are a tightwad, like me, you can get depressed about the budgetary consequences of losing your marbles. According to the Alzheimer's Association,[28] nationwide, we spent up to $236 billion in 2016 to care for Alzheimer's and other dementia patients. On a per-person basis, the total annual healthcare costs in 2015 were $49,126 for Medicare patients with dementia compared to $15,550 for those without the disease.[29] That's right—over three times as much.

There is, however, some good news coming out about the bad news. Recent preliminary reports from a study of 21,000 older adults in the United States concluded that brain health among seniors may be showing some signs of improvement. That study reported in the Journal of the American Medical Association shows that the prevalence of dementia in adults aged 65 and older fell from 11.6% in 2000 to 8.8% in 2012.[30] The study warns that more work needs to be done to confirm these findings, but the authors are guardedly optimistic. The study assigns some of the cause for the favorable trend to broad increases in educational attainment and better control of risk factors that lead to heart troubles. Yes, I said *heart* troubles. It turns out the same habits that are good for the heart are also good for the brain.

The natural tendency for many of us at this point is to say: "What the hell? Do I really want to go to a great deal of trouble pursuing good physical health and longevity if I'm only going to end up spending those extra years locked in the Alzheimer's unit?" The answer is "yes, you do. You really want to fight this." Here are three principal reasons.

1. You may be able to outrun it. The progress in early detection and treatment of cognitive decline and dementia is breathtaking. In fact, recent reports about improvements in brain health seem to describe favorable trends that are picking up speed. In addition, there are a host of promising pharmacological solutions that are in various stages of the approval process. Emerging evidence suggests that both the prevalence and incidence of dementia are declining in first-world countries. With any luck, Alzheimer's will become the polio of the early 21st century, and we can all crow about having whipped it.

2. You can put the odds in your favor. It's like counting the cards at the Blackjack table. You can't guarantee that you will beat the house, but by knowing the rules and keeping track of the cards, you can increase the likelihood that you will be in the group of two out of three who retains mental acuity to the end.

3. You'll enjoy your remaining time more. Much of the stuff that promotes well-being I've already outlined in describing the principles of positive psychology are just the sorts of steps you need to take to lessen the chances of suffering the ravages of dementia. So, it's a twofer—protect your sanity while getting happier. You can't beat that deal.

So what do you have to do? Pretty simple. Follow the four Es: Exercise, eat right, educate, and engage. I know—I'm starting to sound like a broken record. Studies to date suggest that, overall, just about everything that increases your chances of heart disease also raises the chances of dementia. Think bad cholesterol, obesity, smoking, high blood pressure. Most of the recommended lifestyle changes for a healthy heart regimen will include some form of regular exercise and changing your diet to include more fruits and vegetables and less fried food.

The same advice applies to a healthy mind. In fact, a recent study goes even further and finds that exercise is critical even after a diagnosis of Alzheimer's to lessen the effects of the disease.[31] But, increasingly, studies are showing the importance of the other two Es—education and engagement. The National Institute on Aging (NIA) recently initiated a study with the National Academies of Sciences, Engineering, and Medicine to take stock of the current state of knowledge on interventions for preventing cognitive decline and dementia and to help shape the messages NIA conveys to the broader public about these conditions. The Academies' 2017 report summarizes and evaluates the most current scientific research on the topic.[32] The jury is in, and the research shows that social connections and intellectual activity are vitally important factors in lowering the risk of cognitive decline and Alzheimer's.

As it turns out, you may have already made the most important investment in intellectual activity. Studies have been conducted into which factors within our control will lower the odds of dementia and have found a consistent correlation with the number of years of book learning a person has managed to achieve as important markers of mental health. People with more years of formal education (measured by grade level or college attendance) have a lower risk of cognitive impairment later in life than the less-educated.

If you didn't go for that graduate degree, don't despair. It's not too late to get another diploma, all the while increasing your odds at the Alzheimer's table of chance. As Chopra and Tanzi, the authors of *Super Brain*, put it:

> "You can choose to follow an upward learning curve no matter how old you are. By doing so, you will create new dendrites, synapses, and neural pathways that enhance the health of your brain and even help stave off Alzheimer's disease (as suggested by the latest research findings)."[33]

It appears that being a book nerd is important in areas other than those weekend games of Trivial Pursuit.

Beyond diet, exercise, and education, it starts getting a little murky. Studies show that mental and social engagement are also important controllable risk factors for avoiding dementia, but there doesn't seem to be a tested recipe for what works.[34] Researchers have studied subjects who have pursued brain games, volunteer work, and involvement in activities at places of worship. The results seem to show consistently that active lifestyles are preferable to sedentary ones, and that group activities trump solitary pursuits, but the research to date has been inconclusive regarding the optimal path to follow. As one Croatian researcher advises, some tips to maintain brain health include "developing stimulating friendships, continually exposing to new stimulating activities and always trying to get out of the comfort zone."[35]

Some work has shown that the key to activities is purpose. Work conducted by David Bennett, and discussed at some length by Barbara Bradley Hagerty, found that older individuals who can point to their daily objectives are better able to keep their cheese from slipping off the cracker.[36] After doing a series of post-mortem exams, Bennett concluded that these people are far less likely than those with low purpose in life to develop dementia or exhibit cognitive declines, even if their autopsies show that they had the pathology. In fact, people with little purpose were two and a half times more likely to develop dementia than those with a mission.

Whatever the activity, research seems to place a premium on novelty and the evolutionary effect it has on the brain. Much work has been done over the past several years in the field of neuroplasticity, or the ability of the brain to regrow over time and in the right circumstances. Researchers in the field of neuroplasticity have learned that the human brain is a very resilient and developable muscle when it is challenged.

In the treatment of stroke victims, Dr. Edward Taub, a behavioral neuroscientist at the University of Alabama at Birmingham, has made huge strides in using "constraint-induced movement" therapy to encourage stroke patients to regain use of paralyzed limbs. For example, a patient who may have lost use of the left arm has restrictions placed on the use of the right arm over a period of extensive therapy.

Over time, the patient gains gradual use of the left arm. Dr. Taub's research shows that this form of therapy causes the damaged portion of the brain to reprogram its neural hardware to enable use of the affected limb. This regrowth is a form of neuroplasticity.[37]

In much the same way, novelty in lifestyles seems to encourage growth in the brain in ways that fight the effects of aging, including dementia. Unfortunately, other research has shown that the brain's propensity to morph and adapt (for an old dog to learn new tricks, if you will) decreases as you grow old.[38] Perhaps the message here is that the earlier you start your dementia prevention program the better.

One of the most compelling illustrations of the effect that neuroplasticity has on the aging "normal" brain is the oft-cited Nun Study. Beginning in 1986, a young academician at the University of Minnesota, David Snowden, learned of a retirement community of nuns living out their days in Mankato, Minnesota. He was able to convince 678 of these Sisters of Notre Dame to help him with a unique study. The nuns, between ages 75 and 102 at the time, agreed to submit to cognitive tests each year for the rest of their lives. In addition, Dr. Snowden found that many of the nuns had written extensive autobiographical statements in response to a request from the Mother Superior back when they were in their 20s; these statements allowed Snowden to draw some conclusions about the types of psychological makeups that tied to Alzheimer's later in life. Most importantly (and surprisingly), 98% of participants agreed to allow their brains to be autopsied after they died.[39]

While the study is still ongoing, many of the nuns in the study have died and studies of some of their brains have revealed fascinating, and important, evidence of the effects of neuroplasticity. Dr. Snowden found that many of the nuns whose post-mortem brains showed all the pathological signs of Alzheimer's had lived out their lives without signs of dementia. Among the findings were:

- Those who revealed better linguistic abilities in early life were less likely to have dementia later.
- Those who demonstrated positive emotions in early life had greater longevity.
- Low linguistic ability in early life was associated with both dementia in later life and less longevity.

- Higher education in early life was associated with less cognitive decline in later life.[40]

The Nun Study and the works of Drs. Taub and Snowden, as well as many other researchers, hold out much promise that adoption of certain mental activities will help us avoid or compensate for the effects of aging and brain disease. However, reviewers of all of this scientific research have concluded that, while social activities, larger social networks, and a history of social contact can lead to better cognitive function and reduced risk of cognitive decline, the exact type of recommended social engagement is still open to debate.[41] The jury may still be out on precise elements of the best lifestyle to pursue to avoid losing your mind, but there are certain elements that seem to emerge from all of the work done in this area.

In recent years, industries have sprung up around brain training techniques, but the Academy of Science's review of studies on how well the commercial products in this area do the job was inconclusive.[42] Plus, there are some fairly simple, inexpensive and widely available techniques, such as crossword and sudoku puzzles. The trick here seems to be that you shouldn't only play games and you shouldn't play only one kind of game. As they say, variety is the spice of life, and in the effort to keep your mind in shape, variety is essential. The training and activity you undertake should cover memory, reasoning, and speed-of-processing activities.[43] All of these elements affect different domains of the brain.

Some memory gurus suggest learning something new such as a second language or a musical instrument. In fact, any adult education course, particularly in a new field, is worth considering. By playing games that involve teams and/or competitors, you can add a social interaction element to the thinking exercise. The authors of *Super Brain* take the process even further, recommending a broad range of concrete steps that a "mindful memory program" should involve, including enthusiastically learning new things. They advise that you should actively avoid using memory crutches such as lists and that whenever you have one of those brain burps in which you can't recall a familiar name or factoid, you should make the effort and take the few seconds for recall rather than asking your spouse or Siri. They also suggest a wide range of mental exercises to keep a brain fit.[44] Think of it as an aerobic mind workout.

The bottom line is that there are things you can do to reduce the odds that you will end up in the Alzheimer's unit at the retirement home. And it just so happens that many of the activities, habits, and approaches are eerily similar to steps that lead to a sustained state of well-being as suggested by the positive psychologists. There seems to be a pattern developing here...

And keep in mind, not all behavior that appears to be dementia really is.

> *A balding, white-haired man walked into a jewelry store on Friday evening with a beautiful, much younger gal at his side. He told the jeweler he was looking for a special ring for his girlfriend. The jeweler looked through his stock and brought out a $5,000 ring.*
>
> *The man said, "No, I'd like to see something more special."*
>
> *At that statement, the jeweler went to his special stock and brought over another ring. "Here's a stunning ring at only $40,000," the jeweler said.*
>
> *The lady's eyes sparkled and her whole body trembled with excitement. Seeing this reaction, the old man said, "We'll take it."*
>
> *The jeweler asked how payment would be made, and the man said, "By check. I know you need to make sure my check is good, so I'll write it now and you can call the bank Monday to verify the funds; I'll pick the ring up Monday afternoon."*
>
> *On Monday morning, the jeweler angrily phoned the old man and screamed, "Sir... There's no money in that account."*
>
> *"I know," said the old man, "but let me tell you about my weekend."*

4

Spirituality

Woven throughout many of the discussions of, and methods to increase, happiness are a number of topics that involve spirituality. Whether we are discussing Dr. Ryff's definition of personal autonomy or Dr. Seligman's concepts of putting meaning in a "Meaningful Life," or later on when I discuss the keys to resilience, a willingness to look inwardly and apply an overarching set of beliefs is important to achieving a happy life. We all have a set of ground rules we know we should follow, but some of us are better than others at regularly reviewing the rules and making an effort to play by them.

These beliefs may find their roots in an established religion that espouses an all-knowing, everlasting creator, or some other set of unalterable, eternal rules. In other cases, the beliefs may come into play simply through an informal practice of mindfulness and gratitude exercises. While research suggests that some systems of belief provide more psychological support than others during stressful times, the critical value to personal well-being seems to come from the introspective nature of spirituality generally. The term "spiritual" as applied by the researchers is broad and includes the concepts of self-awareness and consciousness. Therein lies some of the difficulty.

If you, the reader, don't like the idea of a self-help book (although you are already pretty deep into this one), then chances are fairly high that you really don't like considering the topic of spirituality. The inward-looking aspect of assessing and correcting your own behavior makes you a little queasy? I feel your pain. I know it's a concept that makes me uncomfortable—on a number of levels.

First of all, it is very personal. At its core, spirituality involves turning inward, taking a look around, and being very honest about what you see, good and bad. There is a reason that confessions are private affairs at church. Because of its personal nature, each party to a conversation about spiritual affairs makes each participant feel ill at ease. I suppose it has a lot to do with the vulnerability that comes with total honesty about your weaknesses and shortcomings.

Moreover, many times, spirituality touches very strongly held beliefs. We all learned the rule that one of the topics that is off-limits in a dinner party conversation is religion. The reason, of course, is that matters that are central to your religion might be anathema to your dinner partner's beliefs. The result is discomfort and disagreement at best, and fisticuffs at worst. In addition, the sales pitch from someone who hopes to convert you to their system of beliefs breeds the same sort of discomfort and anxiety as that caused by a pushy car salesman. Because of the vehemence and awkwardness that the topic engenders, social norms dictate that we should stay away from the subject of religion altogether unless we are in a forum, such as a church, devoted to consideration of the subject.

Second, spirituality is hard to define. Some folks equate the term strictly with religion. Others approach the subject much more broadly and include concepts of self-awareness, consciousness, meditation, and inner peace and harmony. Some folks define it even more broadly to include nature and art. The Association of Medical Colleges opines that spirituality is "expressed in an individual's search for ultimate meaning through participation in religion and/or belief in God, family, naturalism, rationalism, humanism, and the arts."[45] That list sure seems to cover lots of ground.

Third, in part because it is so personal, varied, and squishy, it is also difficult to quantify. A basic tenet of Christianity is that you shouldn't wear your phylacteries broadly on your sleeve, meaning that you should not be ostentatious about your religion.[46] Elsewhere in the Bible, however, believers are admonished not to hide their "candle under a bushel" but to declare their beliefs publicly.[47] In the Buddhist faith, a premium is placed on quiet meditation.[48] In all religions, practitioners can point to others who outwardly (and often loudly) profess adherence to beliefs that don't seem to be reflected in their actual behavior outside of church or temple. Others may go about quietly fulfilling the tenets of their denomination with few outward signs. At the same time, we all probably have friends who profess nonbelief in a divine being but conduct their lives according to a strict code of ethics. Given this range of behavior and behavioral guidelines, how can you measure the amount of spirituality an individual possesses or the effect that it has on the individual's well-being?

An additional complicating factor is that it is often difficult to separate the benefits that may come along with the spiritual enterprise from the benefits that come from the attendant activities. For instance, many times the practice of your religion involves a variety of social aspects. You attend church and see many of your friends there. After church, you hang around for a cup of coffee or a "picnic on the grounds." As I mention in my discussions of positive psychology, dementia avoidance, and resilience, there are health benefits associated with just these sorts of social interactions. Also, your particular flavor of religion may encourage a healthier lifestyle, such as staying away from hard drink and smoke. Those lifestyle choices might lead to a longer life even if you choose to drop out of the church. As another example, for many, the meditative aspects of yoga (in addition to the physical benefits of stretching muscles you didn't even know you had) provide a regular spiritual outlet that is coupled with the social benefits of a group activity. Once again, how do you isolate and measure each of the elements?

Finally, speaking as a red-blooded American male, it is way too touchy-feely. I don't need to get in touch with myself—I know me. I need to just get out there and get'er done. Spirituality is for those who have too much time on their hands and too soft a spot in their psyche. It is for the weak of character—not me and my Type A personality, right?

Wrong. There is a growing body of research that indicates that those who are more spiritual live longer, happier lives, suffer from less depression, and recover more quickly from setbacks, among a host of other benefits.[49] Clearly, touchy-feely comes with benefits. So, now that we've discussed all the issues that make it hard to consider spirituality as a contributor to well-being, let's talk about the reasons that it is important to make the effort.

A fairly extensive body of research concludes that being "spiritual" has a host of attendant mental and physical health benefits. Dr. L sums it up best: "Spiritual people are relatively happier than nonspiritual people, have superior mental health, cope better with stressors, have more satisfying marriages, use drugs and alcohol less often, are physically healthier, and live longer lives."[50] How about that for an all-in-one elixir? In addition, most folks already seem to know this about themselves. According to a recent Pew Research Center poll, the more religious you are, the happier you are with your everyday life.[51]

Deepak and Rudy take it a few steps further in *Super Brain*. They maintain that one of the most powerful ways to promote well-being is to become conscious of "consciousness."[52] After spending many pages promoting the concept that the mind controls the brain, they maintain that the mind can also control reshaping the brain and your personal reality at the same time. Put another way, you are what you feel.

This analysis is pretty deep and philosophical, and smacks (they readily admit) of ancient Far Eastern religious traditions. For the same reasons that you don't discuss religion at dinner parties, I won't get into promoting any spiritual philosophy. Let's just acknowledge that millions (perhaps billions) worldwide go along with the overall idea, and leave it at that. The point is that we need to think about what we are thinking about.

While I concede that there are multiple benefits that can accrue from turning inward, I believe my job here is done. You are now aware that spirituality has a significant upside, separate and apart from eternal life or becoming enlightened. But, in my opinion, you can't fake this stuff. You already have planted inside you some beliefs and precepts that form the basis of your views on right and wrong, eternal life vs. eternal damnation, and gratitude.

It could be that those seeds could use a little watering. You alone know. You have to build on whatever personal variety of spirituality is attractive to you, using the methods that already appeal to you. Listen for your inner voice, and if you don't hear anything, go to another aisle in the self-help section and find a book on "inner voices."

In the meantime, you can always seek out a priest.

Two priests decided to go to Hawaii on vacation. They were determined to make this a real vacation by not wearing anything that would identify them as clergy. As soon as the plane landed they headed for a store and bought some uber-outrageous shorts, shirts, sandals, hats, and sunglasses.

The next morning, they went to the beach dressed in their tourist garb. As they sat in their lounge chairs, enjoying a drink, the sunshine, and the scenery, they noticed a drop-dead gorgeous (and topless) bikini-clad blonde walking straight toward them. They couldn't help but stare.

As the blonde passed them, she smiled and said, "Good morning, Father. Good morning, Father," nodding and addressing them each individually as she passed by.

They were both stunned. How in the world did she know they were priests? So, the next day they went back to the store and bought even more preposterous outfits. Once again, in their new attire, they settled down in their chairs to enjoy the sunshine.

After a little while, the same gorgeous blonde, wearing a different-colored topless bikini, came casually strolling toward them. Again, she nodded to each of them and said, "Good morning, Father. Good morning, Father," and started to walk away. One of the priests couldn't stand it any longer and said, "Just a minute, young lady."

"Yes, Father?"

"We are priests and proud of it; but I have to know, how in the world do you know we are priests, dressed as we are?"

Without hesitation, she replied, "Father, it's me, Sister Kathleen!"

5

I've Got Friends in Flow Places

In his 1922 classic novel about midlife in America, *Babbitt*, Sinclair Lewis writes about the trials and tribulations of George Babbitt as he navigates the waters of being a father and businessman in the mythical mid-size city of Zenith.[53] *Babbitt* has been studied for generations as a commentary on conflicting values of status-seeking, middle class Americans in the Roaring Twenties, but it also gives literary illustration to several of the more important principles of well-being.

In the story, while George finds some success in business, rises through the leadership ranks of the Zenith Booster Club, and takes pleasure in his role as patriarch of the Babbitt family, he finds true happiness in his long and deep friendship with Paul Reisling. When Paul lands in prison after a violent altercation with Mrs. Reisling (as in, Paul pulls out a gun and shoots his wife of many years), George reacts poorly. In the absence of his best friend, Babbitt becomes a wild man, hanging out with loose women and amoral men and participating in activities that shock his friends and family. He thrashes wildly for years trying to find his psychological mooring. For the fictional George Babbitt, and for most of the real-life rest of us, close friends provide much more psychological support than we often give them credit for.

It turns out that research confirms the principle that a close friend and family support group is a key to happiness. The best, and most often cited, validation of this principle has come through the renowned Grant Study, conducted by Harvard University.[54] Starting in 1937, 268 Harvard sophomores from the classes of 1939 to 1944 were recruited to take part in an intense study of the factors that make an individual happy and successful. The group underwent extensive psychological, sociological, medical, and physical testing at the time they joined the study, and have been monitored and retested periodically since.

The study is somewhat unique by virtue of the fact that it has been ongoing now for almost 80 years. As you would expect, the Grim Reaper has taken his toll on the group over the years, but the longevity of the study and ability to retest the subjects over the years has allowed its successive administrators to reach some important conclusions about the effect that various habits of living have on mortality, as well as the secrets of successful living. Researchers have used the data gathered from the participants to make some assessments about how certain life choices and non-negotiables lead to a longer life. But the focus has always been on which life paths lead to happiness.

So what is the bottom line of this 80 years-in-the-making study? If you want one key determinant of happiness, look no further than close friends and family. As summarized by the current director of the Grant Study, Robert Waldinger, in a 2015 TED talk: The happiest and healthiest participants are the ones who maintain close, intimate relationships. Waldinger finds additional support for this proposition in a similar longitudinal study of men from a Boston tenement starting in the 1940s.[55]

What is it about our intimate relationships that promotes our well-being? Put another way, does having a group of close friends improve our chances of getting to the state of "flow" as espoused by Dr. C? "[F]low generally occurs when a person is doing his or her favorite activity—gardening, listening to music, bowling, cooking a good meal. It also occurs when driving, talking to friends, and surprisingly often at work. Very rarely do people report flow in passive leisure activities, such as watching television or relaxing."[56] Thus, to the extent that a supportive group of friends encourages you to engage more in the activities that you enjoy and that lead to flow, it is an effective means to that end.

But as George Babbitt discovered, not all friends are equal in terms of providing psychological and physiological benefits. Babbitt had a large number of "Hail fellow, well met" acquaintances from the Zenith Boosters Club in his friend reservoir, but when his BFF went off to prison to serve a three-year sentence, Babbitt's life drifted until he fell in with a group of heavy drinking, heavy partying, and promiscuous revelers. Only after a wake-up call in the form of a life-threatening illness suffered by his wife did Babbitt return to his established network of family and friends for support.

While Sinclair Lewis no doubt wished to portray other ironies and inconsistencies in Babbitt's life and demeanor when he wrote the novel, it superbly illustrates several points that have emerged from the extensive reported research on the benefits (and risks) that can result from a friends and family network as you grow older. The scientific literature also gives insight into what kind of relationships you need to nurture to sustain your well-being. Dozens of studies have shown that people who have satisfying relationships with family, friends, and their community are happier, have fewer health problems, and live longer. As categorically stated by the National Institutes of Health: Adults who are more socially connected are healthier and live longer than their more isolated peers."[57] All of a sudden you've got another good reason to get together with all those folks you like being around.

George Babbitt's struggles took place in the first half of the 20th century, long before the internet became a ubiquitous feature of our lives. As a result, there is no reference in Lewis' story to social media, no mention of Facebook, no texts or tweets, no posting of pictures on Instagram. Would the presence of electronic communications have materially changed the struggles that George went through? In other words, can we achieve the benefits of social interaction—maintain a group of supportive friends—through the use of social media?

Research on the effects of the sustained use of social media is fairly new and ongoing, but the early results suggest an unsurprising answer to the questions—it depends. At the outset there is little question that the internet has assumed a prominent position in our lives. According to a recent survey by the Pew Research Center 68% of all U.S. adults are Facebook users. Other networking platforms, such as Twitter, LinkedIn, and Pinterest, have less nationwide adoption but cover wide swaths of society.[58] The ramifications of this cultural phenomenon are wide-reaching.

Without question, adding such widely accepted communication methods has some upsides. Increasingly, those looking to establish relationships are employing electronic bulletin boards and dating services to find suitable connections. For shut-ins and those who may have difficulty communicating on a face-to-face basis for whatever reason, electronic messaging provides a convenient means of sending and receiving information. Older people, who may suffer physical limitations, can use the internet effectively to stay connected with family and friends. Social media methods can be used to remove many barriers that can inhibit or prevent communication between people, whether the barriers are physical, geographical, or emotional.

Despite these many benefits much of the public debate recently has tended to focus on some of the negative aspects of social media, both real and perceived. The risks from use of this popular technology include cyber-bullying, threats from sexual predators, the mismanagement of personal information, and the negative impact inappropriate posts and photos can have. Critics also point to the emphasis some sites place on friend counts, which can lead to popularity contests, low self-esteem, anxiety, and depression. Social media have even been accused of encouraging sedentary behavior, with its accompanying health consequences.[59] But what about its effectiveness as a tool for establishing and maintaining friendships?

It turns out that electronic messaging lacks some of the most important characteristics of a real-life conversation. The upside is that a computer does not require cognitive or emotional involvement, making our interaction with it much easier. The bad news is that such dialogue is pretty shallow and one dimensional, even if you are a heavy user of emoticons.

Studies have found that the information conveyed in day-to-day conversations is almost entirely through nonverbal communication.[60] When we interact with others, we are continuously processing wordless signals like facial expressions, tone of voice, gestures, body language, eye contact, and even the physical distance between the participants. These nonverbal signals are the heart and soul of the interaction. We cannot understand the true meaning of an interaction if we do not have the ability to interpret these nonverbal signals. They enable us to infer the other person's intentions, as well as how involved they are in the conversation, whether they are stressed or relaxed, if they are attracted to us, and so on. These messages exist in any type of face-to-face interaction, even those that do not involve active conversation. Nonverbal signals add a level of depth to the interaction, but demand emotional effort.

Psychologists refer to a face-to-face interaction as a "synchronized" form of communication. In such a conversation, we (generally) listen while another person speaks, we nod when others explain, and one knows the other isn't necessarily finished speaking even if they're silent; we can tell when our counterparts are processing information. Synchronized behavior is impossible online, as we cannot see the other online participants in the conversation.[61] The bottom line is that purely online interactions, while they have some value for contributing to well-being, lack many of the attributes, and benefits, of good old-fashioned, honest-to-goodness visits.

As pointed out in the discussions above and below on avoiding dementia and promoting resilience, your social network, whether electronic or flesh-and-blood, is an important contributor to your health. Your friends and family challenge you to stay active and engaged. They also provide critical support when you are on the ropes. Many times, the good that comes from your efforts to be more spiritual is interwoven with the communities that are involved. In each of these cases, substantial research surrounding each of these activities shows that some of the beneficial results are caused by the social webs that you weave and not just a by-product of your efforts.

It is not all good news, however. Once again, Babbitt provides an excellent illustration. George Babbitt's friend Paul landed in the slammer for aiming a gun at his wife and pulling the trigger. He took this course of action (along with multiple extramarital affairs) after years of a contentious relationship in which he felt stressed, put-upon, and henpecked. Were Paul to be tried today, he could stage a defense (probably without success) on the work of several researchers who conclude that there can be a dark side to marriage and friendship.

If the kind of relationship you have with your family looks more like Archie Bunker's than Andy Griffith's, it may cause much more harm than good. Sociological studies have shown that marital strain erodes mental and physical health, and that the negative effect of marital discord on health becomes greater with advancing age.[62] Studies have also shown that the "wrong" kind of friends can be a bad influence on you and your lifestyle. Think smoking, donut-eating, and illicit drugging. (Didn't your mother always tell you to stay away from "those kind" of people?)

The best type of friends to have is also somewhat of a moving, morphing target. Research seems to show that the most beneficial types of friend groups seem to change as you grow older. When you are young, the broader the group, the better, as you experience, and learn, from a wide variety of folks with varying backgrounds. During the career-building, child-rearing, parent-caring years from the ages of roughly 30 to 50, a smaller, more supportive group seems to be best. But all of these needs morph again as you get older, approach and pass into retirement, and begin to develop other physical and mental challenges and needs. As that process unfolds, a wider group of friends seems to provide added benefits for several reasons.

First, a stagnant pool of friends may tend to evaporate as the average age of the group goes up. Health issues (and death) take their toll over time. Retirement itself may cause some of your group to relocate to warmer climes or to the vicinity of grandchildren. Other friends (who have not taken the time to read my advice) as they age may choose a more sedentary, isolated lifestyle, and not be as available as they were in their youth for collegial activities. For whatever reason, you should be mindful of the need to refresh your friend team periodically and maintain a deep bench.

Second, a more eclectic group of friends will help you get your butt off the sofa. As stated by the American Society on Aging: "Social relationships have as much impact on physical health as blood pressure, smoking, physical activity, and obesity..."[63] Your interactions with a broad group of others causes you to get out more, be more active, and try new things.

Not only does this help to combat the tendency to become more sedentary as you grow older, but also it causes you to exercise your most important muscle, your brain. As explained by Dr. Henry Lodge in *Younger Next Year*, physical activity and involvement in life trigger growth messages to your brain and help overcome the decay messages coming from other areas of the body.[64] Once again, this type of positive peer pressure can provide the impetus you need to find and visit those "flow places."

Third, and perhaps most importantly, the wider the group of friends and family, the more you feel that folks have your back. This stress buffering appears to have benefits whether or not those in your network really do plan to support you. Friends tend to take your side in the interpretation of life situations. You overlook their flaws, and they see beyond yours. After all, isn't that one of the primary reasons why you move someone in your personal ledger from the acquaintance column to the friend column?

In addition, if you have need for material support, the wider your group of close friends and family, the more folks you have to turn to for help when the going gets tough. Just knowing that you have a team behind you helps you cope as life throws you curveballs. There even seems to be evidence that you may take better care of yourself if you believe it will allow you to take care of others in your circle.[65]

And guess what—your friends don't necessarily even need to be human. Studies show that the companionship provided by pets can be a boon to our health and happiness. The Harvard Medical School has reported that having a pet—a dog in particular—likely lowers the risk of heart disease.[66] A report by the University of California at Berkeley goes a step further and finds that owning a pet leads to a longer life with less depression and loneliness, higher self-esteem, and improved stress levels.[67] My observation is that pets can also help you make human friends. If you don't believe me, just take a cute puppy on a walk to the park.

The bottom line is this: As you pass into the final third of your life, isolation is bad for you, both mentally and physically. If you are like so many successful professionals and you have allowed your career to consume your life, chances are that one by-product has been a reliance on your job for a big part of your social scene. In fact, you may have achieved so much success that old friends have been left behind. Sometimes, it can indeed be lonely at the top. It is going to take some time and effort to repair this damage.

If one of your goals is to retire, don't forget this part of your plan: You very well may need to think about how to fill the gaps in your schedule, both in terms of activities and participants, after you walk out the door. While it is important to think about what you are going to do, it is also critically important to consider whom you're going to do it with. Just remember—by staying close to a supportive family group and cultivating and refreshing a wide circle of friends, maybe by adding a pet to the mix, you substantially increase the odds that you will live a longer, healthier, and saner life. But you also need to keep in mind that it is important to run with the right people. In case you are wondering, you are too old to start hanging at the dance clubs and using crack cocaine.

And remember, support to and from your friends comes in many different forms.

> *I pointed to two old drunks across the bar from us and told my buddy, "That's us in 10 years."*
>
> *He said, "That's a mirror, you idiot!"*

6

Oh No! Not Another Infomercial About Exercise

I know, I know, you don't need another soul preaching to you about exercise. It's hard to turn on your TV or computer these days without being bombarded with the latest and greatest workout routine or dietary supplement to make your spare tire smaller and your fitness regimen more efficient. Hardly a holiday goes by that there isn't a membership special at your local fitness club/gym. Late night TV "programs" will provide glimpses of lithe bodies selling you equipment or diet pills that will shape you into their likenesses. It's just a guess, but I'll bet you've never met a real person who has gotten rid of their belly fat just by investing in and ingesting a once-a-day, easy-to-swallow miracle caplet.

But there is a great reason that fitness is big business—science has proved that it is the closest thing we have to a silver bullet for good health. Because there are so many sources for information about, and opportunities to pursue, physical fitness, I won't spend much time on the subject. I have little to add, other than a figurative exclamation point and a few salient points that are worth mentioning.

The U.S. Office of Health Promotion and Disease Prevention (OHPDP) has compiled most of the reputable research on the effects of physical activity and concludes that "the benefits of physical activity occur in generally healthy people, in people at risk of developing chronic diseases, and in people with current chronic conditions or disabilities."[68] In other words, just about everybody. In fact, physical activity, especially aerobic activity, is so important that the American Heart Association (AHA) and the American Stroke Association recommend that doctors routinely evaluate their patients' physical activity habits when they come in for routine exams.[69]

While the benefits of regular physical activity accrue to participants of all ages, OHPDP lists several conditions that are of particular application to people as they get to be older. These include lower risk of early death, lower risk of heart disease, lower risk of stroke, lower risk of colon and breast cancers, lower risk of Type 2 diabetes, prevention of falls, reduced depression, and better cognitive function. And as I mentioned earlier in my discussion about increasing the odds of staying mentally healthy, mounting evidence suggests that regular exercise is one of the most effective steps you can take to ward off dementia.

So what kind of exercise are we talking about here? Just about any physical activity will help, whether it is working in the yard or taking the stairs rather than the elevator at work. Research shows that most health benefits occur with at least 150 minutes a week of moderate-intensity physical activity, such as brisk walking, but the more the better. Nevertheless, as both OHPDP and the AHA put it, some physical activity is better than none, so don't forgo the walk or the bike ride just because you don't have time for your full workout.

You hear a lot about "aerobic" exercise being the type of activity with the most benefits. Aerobic exercise refers to activity that requires the body to consume substantially more oxygen than when it is at rest. It is activity that causes the heart to beat faster than usual for a sustained amount of time. How much faster it needs to go depends on the intensity of the activity and, over time, the frequency and duration.

Dig a little deeper (or hang out with buff trainers) and you'll begin to bump into proponents of the benefits of "high intensity interval training" or HIIT. You may see that acronym on the cover of the magazines in your dentist's office. Don't be scared. You can use this term to impress your friends and prove to them that you are serious about your workouts. But, while your reputation as a fitness animal may improve, the research indicates that the health benefits are debatable. You shouldn't be fooled into believing that you have to go to this extreme before you see some good out of exercise.

The research has shown that while the payoffs from physical activity increase when you make the activity aerobic, the total amount of physical activity is more important for achieving health benefits than is any one component, such as frequency, intensity, or duration. For instance, the AHA recommends that everyone reach a minimum of 30 minutes of aerobic exercise five to seven days a week, but the activity can be broken up into 10-minute time periods.[70] As such, taking three brisk walks of 10 minutes each allows you to reach the recommended minimum daily guideline for reducing the risk of heart disease, diabetes, hypertension, and high cholesterol, i.e., the quadrifecta of conditions that could prevent you from winning the lifespan contest.

The key is to find some form of activity that can become a regular and satisfying part of your life. After all, there is a tendency to repeat enjoyable activities, right? Best of all is to find a form of exercise that also allows you to enter that state of flow that causes the time to pass unnoticed. But even if you decide to pursue a passion that doesn't involve physical activity, don't despair. There are a multitude of ways to sneak in habits that work your muscles and race your heart.

If you have been avoiding getting exercise on the grounds that you are too busy, the AHA's factoid on the benefits of just 10-minute excursions into mild activity should settle the internal argument once and for all. Everyone (even you) has 10 minutes to spare, three times a day. Set your wristwatch alarm, and push away from your desk and take a walk around the building or neighborhood, or go get coffee at the Starbucks that is four blocks away instead of the one in your building. Whatever the gimmick you need to play on yourself, put it in motion and get your butt in motion.

Do golf, bowling, tennis, or other recreational sports qualify? How about a good game of corn hole? How about sex? Okay, okay—that last one was just wishful thinking, but the question is do those things you already do for fun get you some physical fitness points? At the risk of sounding harsh, you probably already know the answer here. It depends.

It depends on how much "exercise" is involved, as in getting your heart rate up and sustained at the "up" for a period of time. For instance, if you are playing 18 holes of golf, riding in a cart with a 12 pack of PBR in the basket, maybe not so much. If you replace the riding cart with a pull cart, and trade the beer for a couple of bottles of Gatorade, now you are in business from a cardio standpoint. Carry the bag and the Gatorade…well, you get the picture. Likewise, for tennis. A tough game of singles is going to pay more exercise dividends than a leisurely game of doubles. You know how it works, you get out what you put in, but why not go with an activity that you like. It sure helps when you inject the fitness into the physical that you already enjoy.

For anyone who wants to try to cop out of exercise on the grounds that you are so out of shape that you might hurt yourself—sorry, no dice. OHPDP states categorically in its review of the available research: "The benefits of physical activity far outweigh the possibility of adverse outcomes."[71] That having been said, you will want to bounce your new fitness resolution off of your doctor to make sure there isn't something she hasn't been telling you, and you may want to start slow, but you need to get started. The bottom line—you have no excuse. Turn off the TV, rise up out of the easy chair, and get moving.

Keep in mind the enduring maxim of no pain, no gain…

> *A married couple went to the hospital to have their baby delivered. Upon their arrival, the doctor said he had invented a new machine that would transfer a portion of the mother's labor pain to the baby's father. He asked if they were willing to try it out. They were both very much in favor of it.*
>
> *The doctor set the pain transfer to 10% for starters, explaining that even 10% was probably more pain than the father had ever experienced before. However, as the labor progressed, the husband felt fine and asked the doctor to go ahead and kick it up a notch.*
>
> *The doctor then adjusted the machine to 20% pain transfer. The husband was still feeling fine. The doctor checked the husband's blood pressure and was amazed at how well he was doing. At this point, they decided to try 50%. The husband continued to feel okay. Since the pain transfer was obviously helping the wife considerably, the husband encouraged the doctor to transfer ALL the pain to him.*
>
> *The wife delivered a healthy baby while suffering virtually no pain. She and the husband were ecstatic.*
>
> *When they got home, the mailman was dead on the porch.*

7

Have You Heard the One About...

When you walk into a gathering, whether it is a business meeting or a social get-together, have you ever noticed that you are drawn to the situation in the room that appears to offer humor? Depending on the setting and your familiarity with the other people on hand, the natural tendency will be to join others who are smiling and joking. (And there will be a tendency to avoid suspected or anticipated conflicts.)

I don't know about you, but when I think back on events and situations that I would characterize as "fun," most often laughter was a cause or a natural byproduct. Funny and fun seem to be related somehow. Whether or not laughter actually improves your physical and mental health, it undeniably improves your enjoyment of life. Wouldn't it be nice if you were under doctor's orders to laugh more? Well, here is your prescription—you must incorporate humor into your daily routine for the rest of your life for your benefit and the benefit of others around you.

It turns out that there are tangible benefits to both your mental and physical health resulting from laughter. That's right—a good belly laugh is good for you. With respect to a healthy body, research has shown that laughter boosts immunity to various illnesses, including heart disease,[72] lowers stress hormones,[73] decreases the suffering from emotional pain,[74] and provides muscle relaxation.[75] In addition, among the many health benefits are relief from anxiety and fear,[76] stress relief,[77] mood improvement,[78] and recovery from depression.[79] Laughter increases resilience, and resilient people seem to laugh more.[80] Overall, laughter causes a general increase in personal satisfaction, and it is contagious.

And, if you are uncomfortable in social situations, humor may be the tonic you need to help you. As the Social Anxiety Institute advises: "Laughter is a great antidote to social anxiety. It provides us with physical, psychological, and social benefits, and distracts us from negative thinking habits."[81] Breaking the ice in a conversation may be good medicine for all the participants, even the ones who didn't want to be there in the first place. There is even a scientific term for this—"eustress." According to Dr. Lee Berk, associate professor at Loma Linda University, "[L]aughter appears to cause all the reciprocal, or opposite, effects of stress."[82]

In case you're not yet convinced, there are also a host of studies that indicate that laughter causes your brain to release beta-endorphins, a morphine-like compound that creates a sense of euphoria. But the benefits have been shown to go beyond a temporary "runner's high." A group of researchers recently released a study that found that the endorphins that come along with laughter can combat the chronic release of cortisol in the brains of older people. Cortisol is a chemical that impairs the ability to learn and sustain memory. The study found that humor can be used to promote learning ability and combat delayed recall—and it's one kind of treatment that is enjoyable to all.[83]

While there is some debate whether the benefits of laughter are enduring or simply momentary shots of endorphins, there seems to be no downside (other than the embarrassment that comes along with laughing so hard you wet your pants). Dr. Robert Provine, in his 2001 book, *Laughter: A Scientific Investigation*, suggests that studies showing long-term benefits from laughing have suffered from methodological flaws that failed to adequately separate the effects of the laugh from other factors, such as the social interaction that accompanies the laughter. (If given the chance, I'd like to suggest to Dr. Provine that it is somewhat self-defeating to try to separate social interaction from laughter, as I have found laughter to bring about the interaction as well as causing its stress-relieving effects.) Dr. Provine does concede that the short-term benefits of a good laugh are undeniable. In fact, he cites the best example of the therapeutic use of laughter as its use in pain management for cancer patients.[84]

Okay, so now I've convinced you that you need to laugh more and you want to inject some humor into your life, but how do you go about it? Humor is a lot trickier than it used to be, especially in the workplace. Political correctness seems to have outlawed all but the tamest of jokes. The Human Resources Department constantly reminds us that we must display "sensitivity" in all our utterings. My observation is that it is the rarest of jokes that won't be deemed offensive by someone. As a result, we have been conditioned to believe that any humor in the workplace is dangerous.

Moreover, because of the liability attached to "hostile" workplaces and because some jokes can be taken as a form of sexual harassment, we have reverted to the least common humor denominator at the office. We have been trained to examine all that we think, do, or say to imagine if anyone could possibly take offense at it, and avoid such a result. In many cases, we have trained ourselves to believe, when in doubt, don't spit it out. While this may have forced some to move on to find something else to complain about, it certainly has cut down on the circulation of good jokes. So, what to do?

Don't despair. You may spend most of your waking hours in the humor-barren workplace, but with any luck that is going to change as you work to replace work and workplace with something else. If you don't think that "something else" includes enough laughter, there are several strategies to pursue. First, actively seek out humorous activities. Watch funny movies. Go to comedy clubs. Find the blog of a comedian you like. Do something silly. Read the funnies in the newspaper. Create a file on your computer (depending on the variety of humor you prefer, you might consider keeping the file on your home computer) to keep the jokes and stories that make you laugh, and get in the habit of going there when you need a boost. By having humor be one of the criteria you use in choosing an activity, you not only enjoy the health benefits inherent in laughing but also are more likely to stick with it.

Second, seek out funny friends and encourage them to make you laugh (and return the favor). Granted, political correctness has never been my strong suit and I am not the best proponent for the humorless work environment. When I participated in my bank's sensitivity training several years back (mandatory for everyone, including the president), I made clear to the group to which I was assigned that no joke was too offensive for my ears. It got me a lot of good new material, but I also understand that not everyone feels the same way and that I can't assume that my co-workers (or my social acquaintances) share my no-holds-barred approach to jokes.

Humor is highly subjective, and appearances and relationships must be maintained. Moreover, civility demands that you not be offensive to those around you. But it is important to keep in mind the benefits that we can all enjoy if we lighten up a little, and seeking out those connections who feel the same way is a key to injecting giggles into your gut.

Third, try to find the humor in every situation. I realize that it is the epitome of bad taste to laugh out loud at a funeral (or other serious occasion), but finding the humor in a situation can often turn distress into eustress. The studies on resilience indicate that one of the keys to rebounding from bad life events is to find a way to laugh about the predicament. Of course, depending on the circumstances, you might be best off to reach out to one of your funny friends (and not that sourpuss next to you) to express your humorous insights.

Finally, as with other areas of your life, take control of the humor issue. Even if you have always considered yourself to be too serious to fall prey to a sense of humor, don't give up. The studies show that humor can be learned. Here's an experiment—go to a joke website, and find three jokes that make you laugh. The next time you are around close friends, tell the jokes. See which one works best. Put a mental sticky note on that one. The next time you are at a gathering of acquaintances, tell that joke. I'll bet it will trigger others to tell their favorites and everyone will get a dose of endorphins. If not, what have you lost?

Just to make it easy on you, here's a start.

> *Two little kids are in a hospital, lying on stretchers next to each other outside the operating room, the first surgeries of the day. The first kid leans over and asks, "What are you in here for?"*
>
> *The second kid says, "I am getting my tonsils out, and I am afraid."*
>
> *The first kid says, "You've got nothing to worry about. I had that done when I was four. They put you to sleep, and when you wake up they give you lots of Jell-O and ice cream. It's a breeze."*
>
> *The second kid then asks, "What are you here for?"*
>
> *The first kid says, "Circumcision."*
>
> *"Whoa!" the second kid replies. "Good luck, buddy. I had that done when I was born. Couldn't walk for a year."*

While we are on the topic:

> *Do you know what you call a cheap circumcision?*
>
> *A rip-off.*

And (I can get away with this only because I am current on my dues to the American Bar Association):

> *Did you hear about the lawyer who was too big to fit in a coffin?*
>
> *They gave him an enema and buried him in a shoebox.*

8

Resilience, or No Excuses

So the thought may be crossing your mind: Why do we need to spend time thinking about resilience? Isn't that something you either have or you don't, and what's it got to do with happiness anyway? So let's start with a fairly depressing line of thought just to ruin your day. You remember the pithy saying from years back: "Today is the first day of the rest of your life." While that is, of course, true, there is a flip side to the album: "All the bad things that will happen to you before you die lie before you, and they are being jammed into an increasingly small amount of time." Stated another (and equally uplifting) way, as you get into your twilight years, shit seems to happen more and more often. Our bodies age, our brains shrink, and our friends and loved ones move away or just move on to the final rodeo.

We may be taking all the recommended steps to ensure the maximum levels of well-being in our lives, and we keep getting knocked to our knees by bad news. And it is not just the latest notice of another upcoming memorial service; our biannual checkups with the doctor have moved past annual reoccurrence to a recommendation of semiannual frequency, and the list of "issues" to bring to the attention of the physician keeps getting longer. More and more of your conversations over coffee seem to dwell on new medications. Oh, and your old golfing (or bridge, or Thursday night dinner, or whatever) companion just moved to North Carolina to be closer to the grandkids.

Now, you may be thinking that many of the steps recommended in the preceding chapters are designed to help mitigate some of the bad stuff life throws at us. The regular physical activity helps prevent the bad news at the doctor's office. The increased social activities provide an ever-evolving friend group to fill in unexpected gaps. An increased focus on spirituality gives me more tools for coping with adversity. And you now know how important it is to find humor in every situation, even those that require the darkest humor to find a smile. In addition, you are working hard to find the bright side of every situation. Even with all of these tools in your tool belt, however, life will find a way to hammer you and you will have to find it within yourself to recover from the misfortune. That is where resilience comes in.

As I began to focus on the subject, I learned that there is a surprising amount of divergence in the literature about how to promote resilience, or even what it means. To the untrained ear, it can get mighty confusing. Take this explanation from a recent paper by R. A. Cummings and M. Wooden: "[R]esilience is the power of homeostasis, first to retain control of SWB [subjective well-being] and, second, to restore the dominance of HPMood [homeostatically protected mood] following excursion of the affective experience outside the 'attractor region' (set point range). As a consequence of retained homeostatic control, and provided that respondents are operating within their set-point-range at baseline, the addition of weak resources or challenges to their life will normally have little impact on measured levels of SWB."[85] Huh?

Fortunately, Drs. Cummings and Wooden start their article with a definition of resilience that even I can understand, taken from Merriam-Webster: "an ability to recover from or adjust easily to misfortune or change."[86] This definition puts the concept in a fairly simple and, frankly, antiseptic context. The National Multiple Sclerosis Society uses similar simple terms to describe resilience: "the ability to solve problems and bounce back from difficult situations." Resilience for people who suffer from MS is important because they face a disease that attacks the central nervous system and often leads to progressively disabling physical conditions. The MS Society focuses on resilience as an effective means of coping with the challenges of the disease.[87]

The Society's resource materials recognize that some of the members of the general population have better built-in levels of resilience than others. Much like the factory settings for happiness, some folks bounce back more quickly than others. When dealing with MS, the Society counsels folks with the disease not to assume that they have no control over their own resilience quotient—they refer to it as the resilience "muscle" and recommend that their constituents go to the effort to exercise and strengthen this muscle. The Society's website cites research that life satisfaction can be more positively affected by resilience than by physical functioning.[88]

Similarly, Jim Rimmer, Director of the National Center on Health, Physical Activity and Disability, has studied the factors that are critical to living a satisfying life following an injury or disability such as a debilitating spinal cord injury. Dr. Rimmer's research has found that one of the most important factors in recovery is resilience. He has observed that in many cases there is a tendency following an injury or disability for the individual to engage in "morbid rumination." In such circumstances, the individual replays over and over in his or her mind "could have/should have" types of mind games that ultimately lead to additional physical and psychological health problems.

To prevent or minimize morbid rumination and get the individual on the road to enjoying a fulfilling life, Rimmer recommends three key habits for promoting resilience: mindfulness, exercise, and good nutrition. His studies and those of his colleagues show that those who focus on these three elements are more likely to have a higher quality of life and bounce back from a wide range of injuries, diagnoses, and disabilities. It's kind of like a how-to for playing the hand when life deals you really crappy cards.

But what about taking it to the extreme? What about resilience after facing life-or-death situations and nonstop stress? This scenario is precisely the challenge that Gen. George Casey took on when he became Chief of Staff of the U.S. Army.

General Casey had led the multinational force in Iraq and had witnessed a troubling aftermath to the service that many soldiers had performed in that conflict and other deployments overseas. He was disturbed by the increases in the number of diagnoses of post-traumatic stress disorder (PTSD) and the rise in suicides of soldiers both in combat zones and after returning home. As he looked into the programs and training offered by armed services, he realized that a good deal of attention was being paid to soldiers and vets after being diagnosed with PTSD, but that far too little attention was being paid to bolstering the psychological well-being of all soldiers. There was essentially no training to make soldiers and their families more psychologically robust, thereby helping them weather difficulties, regardless of the source. As he puts it, the Army developed "a resiliency program that shows promise for [the Army's] workforce and its support network so our soldiers can 'be' better *before* deploying to combat so they will not have to 'get' better *after* they return."[89]

How did the Army go about this? First they recruited one of the nation's premier researchers on resilience, Dr. Martin Seligman from the University of Pennsylvania, to develop a soup-to-nuts program to test and train for resilience. The program was aptly named the Comprehensive Soldier Fitness program, or CSF. You may remember Dr. Seligman's name from Chapter 2. In addition to his renown in the field of resilience, he is one of the most highly respected authorities on positive psychology and well-being. In light of that, it probably comes as no surprise that Doc Seligman adapted his PERMA model to come up with a suitable program.

Accordingly, the CSF test for resilience (of course, the Army has a fancy name for it—Global Assessment Tool, or GAT) focuses on four aspects of the soldier's psychological readiness: emotional, familial, social, and spiritual fitness.[90] Once the GAT identifies the soldier's strengths and the areas that can use improvement, the CSF offers optional training in each of the four tested areas designed to address deficiencies, and a mandatory course on post-traumatic growth. The CSF also established a program designed to train sergeants by helping them understand resilience and then pass on the knowledge across the Army. Those who complete the program are designated Master Resilience Trainers. The Army has trained over 45,000 MRTs since 2009. Additionally, over five and a half million soldiers, civilians, and family members have taken the GAT. General Casey proudly points to the CSF as one of the finest pieces of his prodigious legacy.

The importance of resilience is not limited to the Army. The trials and tribulations of everyday life occur whether or not you served in the military or have ever done a stint in a war zone. As we get older, the stresses in our life evolve, but they continue and the need for resilience continues as well. As Hara Marano, Editor-at-Large of *Psychology Today*, puts it in her article on "The Art of Resilience": "Resilient people do not let adversity define them. They find resilience by moving forward to a goal beyond themselves, transcending pain and grief by perceiving bad times as a temporary state of affairs."[91] Dr. Marano and others have come up with traits to cultivate in order to bolster your level of resistance. Each researcher seems to describe these traits in different ways, but they generally come down to some bedrock principles that look a lot like the elements of the Army's GAT:

1. Maintenance (and use) of a supportive social network
2. Cultivation (and use) of good self-care habits (think diet, a good night's sleep and exercise)
3. Retention of a sense of meaning, purpose, and growth
4. Paying attention to some religious or spiritual proclivities that provide some moral guideposts
5. Staying mentally active and aware
6. Maintaining realistic optimism

To this list, the MS Society would add mindfulness meditation, practicing gratitude, knowing when to let go, practicing forgiveness, and focusing on those elements of resilience that you enjoy and come naturally to you.[92]

If all of this sounds familiar, there is a reason. As General Casey and the U.S. Army learned, many of the same habits that seem to make you resilient are the same or similar to the ones that contribute to happiness, and vice versa. People who rank high on the measures of psychological well-being are, by and large, more resilient. As it turns out, resilience and well-being are closely aligned. And the literature seems to single out a couple of these factors as particularly critical for maximum resilience: optimism and social support.[93]

Let me offer a case in point: Paul Ware, my friend and former law partner. On the morning of October 15, 2014, Paul was in his car on his way to the office. At 53, Paul was at the height of his career as the head of the mergers and acquisitions practice of a large regional law firm. Although he enjoyed some of life's indulgences, including an occasional cheeseburger, he was no slouch. He was an accomplished bike rider having finished many charity bike rides exceeding 100 miles in distance and some stretching over multiple days.

However, on that fall day in his car, as he approached downtown, he sensed that something was wrong. When he started his short 12-minute commute all was well, but as he approached the red light at 21st Street and Highland Avenue, he was unable to lift his left foot to engage the clutch, and his car stalled at the intersection. Still having his wits about him, Paul first telephoned his wife, who didn't answer. The next call was to his assistant at the office. By now, he had to report that his left arm also wasn't working. The assistant was able to locate Paul's wife, who promptly called 911 for an ambulance to take him to the hospital.

By the time Paul arrived at UAB Hospital, he had lost the use of the entire left side of his body. The doctors soon diagnosed his condition as a very serious "brain bleed" in the right side of his brain. In everyday parlance, he had had a stroke. In Paul's words, his brain blew up. Most of us have had exposure to stroke victims and know how debilitating the aftermath can be. Usually, however, we think of strokes as striking older folks. Fifty-three seems awfully young for a stroke (particularly for those of us who have passed that age). Equally disturbing was the suddenness and absence of any warning.

In Paul's case, the early prognosis was not good. He had lost complete use of his left arm and his left leg. His speech was somewhat slurred. His future was cloudy.

But Paul also had many things working in his favor. First and foremost, he had the support of his wife of 30 years, Joanna, and his grown children. To back up his caring family was a huge circle of caring friends. Fortunately for Paul, he lives in Birmingham, Alabama, with its thriving medical community and a research facility that includes specialists in the treatment of strokes. While the stroke snatched some of his mobility, it did not lessen one of Paul's signature strengths—a positive attitude. He didn't dwell on the misfortune that had landed in his lap (or more accurately, his left). He did not start his own pity party. From the moment that he pulled over on the side of the road to call for help, he has approached his condition with a matter-of-fact but optimistic mindset. In addition, he has retained his wonderfully dry, but outrageously offbeat, sense of humor.

So how has he dealt with his neurological challenge? He immediately started an aggressive regimen of physical therapy. In order to devote the time needed to fully combat his new condition, he decided to retire from his law practice. His recovery has been slow but steady, and, as he has managed to gain more and more mobility (and, thus, independence), he has returned to one of his old passions, painting. Throughout his legal career, Paul had used what little spare time he could grab to apply brush to canvas. His artist's eye did not abandon him when his brain shut down some of his limbs.

Now, Paul spends his days not in a law office but in the studio he shares with a couple of other artists with a paintbrush in his good hand. Paul says: "Having a place to go every day, a routine, and a productive, creative outlet is very important to my recovery and state of mind. It is structured and disciplined, even though self-imposed rather than driven by clients and professional demands. This routine is pretty central and defining now." These days, Paul can be found in his studio—at least you can find him there when he is not on his bicycle.

Soon after he started therapy, Paul found a way to return to his favorite form of exercise—cycling. Instead of his old wheels, he bought a recumbent bike and found someone who could adapt it for his recovering but still weakened left side. Gradually, his stamina on the bike improved and he could keep up with some of his old biking group.

A few months into this routine, on a sunny afternoon, Paul was riding with a friend a few miles from his home when a woman in a car ran through a stop sign directly into his path. Despite his quick reaction, he flipped his bike trying to avoid a collision, and he was back on his way to the hospital, this time with a concussion and cracked ribs. Down and out? Not on your life. A week later, he was back on the bike and in the market for a faster set of tires. His rationale: "If I had been going faster, I would have made it through the intersection before that car pulled out." In September 2015, barely 11 months after his stroke, Paul rode 70 miles over two days in the Multiple Sclerosis Ride for the Cure in the Florida Panhandle. He raised almost $4,600 for the ride, which he equates with a dollar for every person in Alabama diagnosed with MS. At the awards banquet following the event, he received a standing ovation and a special presentation—the "Back in the Saddle" award. In 2016, he rode more than 95 miles in the event, and his goal for 2017 is to complete the full 150-mile course.

(As an aside, I rode with Paul a few weeks before the 2016 MS 150 event, thinking cockily that I would have no trouble keeping up with a stroke victim on a funny-looking three-wheeled contraption. Wrong! Despite taking mercy on me and pursuing a leisurely pace, Paul wore me out. I dropped out after 7 miles. He completed a 25ish-mile workout with no signs of fatigue.)

I asked Paul recently about the changes in his life since his stroke, and, in particular, whether he misses his legal practice. He says he misses the interaction with his fellow lawyers, but not the work. In fact, he says he now has the time to enjoy an active social life. Before his stroke, some of his friends used to refer to his wife, Joanna, as the "Widow Ware" because she attended so many events without Paul. He always seemed to be at the office in those days. Now, he is able to enjoy his large group of friends and strengthen those relationships.

Going back to the simple definition of resilience set out by Merriam-Webster: "an ability to recover from or adjust easily to misfortune or change," Paul would probably take issue with any characterization of what he has been through since his stroke as an easy adjustment. He would also quickly inform Mr. Webster that this recovery is a work in progress, not a thing of the past. But here is the kicker: Paul says he has "never been happier." His ongoing recovery epitomizes this concept of resilience. In my book, his determination to participate in long distance bike riding fund-raisers also qualifies him as the embodiment of grit, or the drive that keeps you on a difficult task over a sustained period of time.

So what are the lessons to take away from Paul's experience? Shit happens, and it tends to happen when we least expect it. What we do with it is up to us. The principles of positive psychology and the path to well-being don't change under lousy circumstances. Studies on resilience bear this out. In fact, the rapidly developing study of the effects of resilience on well-being seem to point out that it is a two-way street. Those who rank high on well-being scales are more resilient to the bad things that life throws their way.[94] But it also seems that being more resilient is one of the causes of subjective happiness, particularly in retirement.[95]

The bottom line is this: Resilience and happiness are interwoven, bad things are gonna happen, and they're likely gonna happen more often as we get older. The more we focus on general principles of well-being, we will also be cultivating resilience, which will help further promote being happy. If you don't believe it, call Paul.

Now, here's a story about the outer limits of resilience and adapting to new challenges.

Upon hearing that her elderly grandfather had just passed away, Katie went straight to her grandparents' house to visit her 95-year-old grandmother and comfort her. When she asked how her grandfather had died, her grandmother replied, "He had a heart attack while we were making love on Sunday morning." Horrified, Katie told her grandmother that two people each nearing 100 years old having sex would surely be asking for trouble.

"Oh no, my dear," replied Granny. "Many years ago, realizing our advancing age, we figured out the best time to do it was when the church bells would start to ring. It was just the right rhythm. Nice and slow and even. Nothing too strenuous, simply in on the ding and out on the dong."

She paused to wipe away a tear, and continued, "He'd still be alive today if that ice-cream truck hadn't come along."

9
Pulling It All Together

Like a televised sporting event, it is time to do a halftime recap of this game. We determined at the kickoff that the vast majority of us have the same overarching goals as we enter the next (and final) leg of our lives: We would like to have maximum enjoyment of the time we have left with our minds and bodies intact to the greatest extent possible. Thus far, we have discussed happiness/well-being, mental health (as in, dementia prevention), physical health, and resilience. Let's review the highlight films and list the lifestyle elements that research shows us are important to each:

Happiness (borrowing from Doc Seligman)
    Positive emotions
    Engagement
    Relationships
    Meaning
    Accomplishments

Mental marble retention
    Social engagement
    Mental engagement
    Exercise
    Diet

Resilience
    Supportive social networks

Self-care habits
Meaning, purpose, and personal growth
Spirituality
Mental activity
Optimism

Physical fitness
Just about anything that regularly gets your heart rate up

It doesn't take a genius to figure out some recurring and overlapping themes here.

Also, for most of us, there are no real surprises. Most, if not all, of these elements, were covered in the first six weeks we were a Boy/Girl Scout (which, by the way, is about as far as I made it). You might say that this is an extension of the "Everything you need to know, you learned in kindergarten" school of thought. If so, we can consider this a preschool refresher course, but we need to realize that the stakes are just as high in the third third of life as they were for the first tenth. The hope would be that we picked up some pointers along the way that will make the learning process a little easier this go 'round and that there will be a little less drama (and tears) in the sandbox.

So, what do we do with this stuff now that we have discovered it? Remember how I started this tome—I'm on this road trip, this journey to figure out what to do next, what to do with what's left of my life. It just so happens that I have been casting about trying to come up with some activities in which to engage—some passions to pursue—once I hang up my career. In this process, I have asked dozens of others what they are doing, or plan to do, or would do differently, in retirement.

The responses I have heard have ranged across the board. Many people I have spoken with have been content to let life simply unfold after retirement. Often, I have been told, somehow the calendar just fills up with "stuff." You sleep a little later, you take your time with the daily chores—"Don't ever do two chores on one day, spread 'em out." You watch that talk show in the afternoon. Regular naps. More mystery novels. Baths instead of showers. In some ways, it seems like the direct inverse of the life of a young working mother, where every minute of every day is honed to razor-sharp efficiency.

Other acquaintances have chosen activities, some that I would describe as passions, that fill the time and provide satisfaction on some level. In this group I include my friends who have undertaken regular, significant volunteer activities as well as those who play regular and sustained recreational sports such as golf or tennis. No question that such pursuits seem to check more of the boxes than the taking-life-as-it-comes approach. But I had to wonder if that path was the best for me given what I am hoping to achieve.

Still others have taken a more measured approach. They, like I, have wondered if pursuit of some activities are more beneficial than others and whether there is anything to be gained by planning at all. If the material offered up in the preceding umpteen pages has failed to convince you of the merits of thinking this mind-teaser out, once again, I invite you to bail before you waste any more time. If not, come along with me as I undertake to examine five potential courses in light of all I've discovered in this process so far.

I have attempted to assess the merits of some representative options against the principles that I have discussed in the preceding chapters. I have learned in this process that regardless of whether I am seeking well-being or a nimble mental state, or a good short-term memory, or to bounce back from adversity if/as I become a sexa-, septua-, octo-, and nonagenarian, there are some basic rules I need to follow to improve my odds of living a happy remainder of my life. Of course, it is one thing to know what the rules are and it is an entirely different animal to apply and follow the rules. Let's not forget that we are all human. To that end, unless we honestly enjoy the activities we target, regardless of the personal benefit, it is unlikely that we make and take the time to pursue them.

Since all of the people who have devoted their lives to the study of positive psychology and active brains seem to have come up with lists of activities to promote wellness and catchy anagrams to make their advice memorable, I have decided to craft my own scale for evaluating activities I will take under consideration. For ease of remembering (since remembering is one of the goals), I call it the SCALES scale.

The elements of the SCALES scale are as follows:

Social interaction
Concentration, in the form of brain stimulation
Accomplishment, in the form of setting and striving for a goal or a result
Laughter, in the form of fun and enjoyment
Exercise, in the form of some physical exertion
Spirituality

Catchy, huh? My plan is to use the SCALES scale as the common lens through which to assess the widely divergent activities I will explore in Part II of this book. But it is not without coincidence that the rungs of the SCALES scale fall in the order that they do.

Social networks are at the top of the list. The level and quality of your interaction with family and friends has far-reaching consequences as you grow older. As discussed in the prior chapters, the first S in the SCALES scale affects your health, both physical and mental, and your ability to bounce back from the setbacks that you will inevitably encounter. For all of us, the quality of our social interactions will depend on the level of life support that comes along with it.

Being in a football stadium with 105,000 other fans may provide a good deal of interaction with others, but the experience provides little benefit other than getting you out of the house to witness a ball game. A book club meeting, on the other hand, goes beyond discussion of the ideas in the book to interactions of a personal nature, and collaborative efforts to solve personal issues. In addition, at least for me, an element of desirable social interaction is the degree to which my spouse can (and would want to) join me. You may feel that spousal separation is a plus—a variation on the "I married him for life, but not for lunch" theme. But others may want activities that work well for a twosome.

"Concentration" runs the risk of being a little scary. The point here is that we shouldn't fill our lives with totally mindless activities and expect the muscle between our ears to stay in good shape. Brain stimulation is critical to keeping your mental marbles polished. But, we shouldn't play brain games all of the time to the exclusion of the other elements of happiness. The key here, and a theme that runs throughout the research, is that success in retirement depends on not retiring from life and mental challenges.

But it is a new kind of challenge. Having an objective or goal tied to your activities is the key to losing yourself in your activity and achieving personal satisfaction—reaching the state described as "flow." The purpose that comes with the activity gives us a reason to get out of bed and get back in the game. As Barbara Bradley Hagerty puts it, you need something that is unique, challenging, and interesting to maintain the commitment.[96]

Laughter is a placeholder for the emotion that we intrinsically know as "fun"—think of the squeals you hear near the merry-go-round at the playground and you get the picture. Without question, however, fun is a very subjective concept. To extend the previous imagery a little, some kids find riding a merry-go-round to be nauseating. Only you know what floats your boat, but, as a rule, if you enjoy an activity you are more likely to engage in it. Enjoyment is, after all, an overarching goal of this whole exercise. That having been said, it is important that having fun not be the be-all and end-all of your ambitions. It is a key to making sure that I will pursue an activity in the first place and that I will stick with it.

Enjoyment is also somewhat elusive. An activity may always involve concentration and social interaction but may not always be fun, or may become less fun as it becomes routine. I believe you must constantly ask yourself if you are still having fun, and how to keep it fresh. Laughter is a tricky one.

Physical activity and spirituality, as mentioned in the chapters covering those topics, are largely outside the scope of this book, but that doesn't mean they are unimportant. As a result, while they rate more than an honorable mention on the SCALES scale, they are somewhat secondary to the SCAL pieces. One way of looking at it is that an activity that scores high in the first four elements is made even better if it includes elements of exercise and spirituality.

Also, diet is an important factor that has myriad effects on our well-being, but it's covered, *ad nauseum*, in other media. For purposes of evaluating an activity, I view the effects that the activity may have on a healthy diet as being part and parcel of the exercise score. But the good thing about exercise and spirituality is that there are ways to add these elements to virtually any other passion you choose to pursue.

For example, nothing stops a serious devotee to the game of chess from adding a meditative gratitude session and 30-minute jog to an otherwise chess-focused routine.

The observant reader will note some apparent missing considerations in the SCALES scale, such as personal autonomy, self-acceptance, and environmental control, as well as the important roles they play in the pursuit of happiness. Subsumed within these topics are gratitude for all the blessings we enjoy, not the least of which is having enough mental wherewithal to go through this process in the first place. Also, apparently missing is the need to be able to shake off and get beyond our stumbles and wrong turns. Getting beyond the pileups in life often requires forgiving myself, as well as dropping grudges and forgiving others.

All of these elements are important and are imbedded in the principles of well-being going back to Carol Ryff's early works. While they do not appear on the surface of the SCALES scale, I consider those qualities to be important (and in some cases difficult) overlays to the approach of any activity I choose to pursue. The objective here is to develop a template for evaluating the efficacy of possible pursuits in the "next life" in the context of improving my odds for a long, healthy tenure. Suffice it to say that autonomy, self-acceptance, and control of surroundings are principles that must be considered in arriving at grades for each of the SCALES elements. Let's just call them some of the basic rules of the road—kind of like following the speed limit, sometimes you don't exactly follow the letter of the law.

Ms. Observant will also notice that I have not mentioned that some activities provide more social benefit than others. This factor is what Doc Seligman maintains will take you from the Good Life to the Meaningful Life. Such intangibles as the warm fuzzies you get from doing good works should not be discounted, but I have tried to avoid the subjective judgments that must accompany the valuation of such activities. For me, my assessment of the value of my activity that accrues to others will be an important factor in determining the spirituality score that I come up with for that pursuit.

As you ponder my methodology, you may be wondering: Where did the "flow" go? While I buy into Dr. C's theory that flow is an important consideration, I view it more as an end than as a means. If we are scoring high on SCALES, we will experience varying degrees of flow along the way—we will be content with the activities we pursue, losing all track of time. In other words, we will be happy (and hopefully live longer and with fewer brain farts).

So, we have come up with a list of factors and we have them ranked; should we assign some values? Of course we should. Don't we all love having the ability to assign numerical rankings to stuff? We want to know the score of the game, the ranking of the team, the place of anything on any list. And each of us probably wants to tinker with the weightings. For instance, laughter is important to me, and probably more important than it is to most other people. I am also anxious to de-emphasize accomplishment in the next phase of life. So, for my purposes, I like the following matrix—the first element, social interaction, given its importance, gets a 30% weighting. The next three letters of the scale (concentration, accomplishment, and laughter) get 25%, 15% and 20% weightings, respectively. And exercise and spirituality each get 5%. I will assign a score between 1 and 10 to each letter on the scale and the result will be a score that will allow me to rank each activity. Oh hell, why not?

For those of us who rely on spreadsheets for everything, a sample matrix to arrive at a composite score for a fictional pursuit (using my subjective weightings) would look like this:

Factor	Score	Weighting	Weighted Score
Social Interaction	9	30%	2.7
Concentration	6	25%	1.5
Accomplishment	7	15%	1.1
Laughter	7	20%	1.4
Exercise	3	5%	0.2
Spirituality	5	5%	0.3
Composite		100%	7.1

In theory, at least, the composite score that results for this possible passion can be compared to the composite scores from others and a "winner" will be declared.

Immediately, because you are smart and analytical, you are thinking, "How do you come up with the scores to input into the SCALES scale matrix?" This is where the side trips on the long road trip come in. You are going to have to do some research. In order for the composite score to have any validity, you need to know enough about the proposed pursuit to make some sort of educated judgment about the score to assign to each of the factors. You're gonna have to try it out. You don't need to commit yet, but you do need to do more than just dip your toe in the water.

Fortunately for me, this whole quantification endeavor has a lot of appeal. You may recall that when I took Dr. L's test for which happiness exercises suit me, I scored highest on: "Doing more activities that truly engage you: Increasing the number of experiences at home and work in which you 'lose' yourself, which are challenging and absorbing (i.e., flow experiences)." That may explain why I am willing to try this stuff, but what doesn't fit into my personality is strapping a process around my activities to make the evaluation. I'm way too spontaneous for that, right? Then, I step back and realize that it is just that sort of spontaneity that has pushed me in directions, sometimes gotten me in trouble, in the past and that I am trying to avoid this time around. The SCALES scale gives me the tools; now I just need the self-discipline to apply them and keep track of the results.

So what are the activities to which I should apply the scale? This has been a much longer process than I would have imagined. Over the past three years I have developed a list of over 75 possible pursuits. The list continues to emerge and evolve as I have more conversations with people who seem to be satisfied with their lives and lifestyles. At one point, it became apparent that the list involved not only activities that could be described as possible "passions" but also some that were better described as pleasant "diversions." This realization led to a bifurcation of the list into two. By way of example, a couple of the items that I relegated to the diversion list were golf and travel.

The list of possible passions was pared further just by applying the appeal test—if the activity didn't have any appeal to me from the get-go, it fell to the bottom of the page. Quilting, for example, may be a great pastime that could score high on the SCALES scale, but it has no appeal for me. Others got tossed due to reasons of personal safety. Flying lessons, for instance, got axed because my wife convinced me that my short attention span did not mix with this activity and could lead to premature death. (I disagree, by the way, but the consequences of error on my part outweighed the need to repair my damaged pride.)

Finally, I applied a rule that the activity couldn't be one that I already pursue. Exclusion of the familiar is my attempt to realize the healthy brain benefits that come along with getting out of your comfort zone to try something new. Given that one of the reasons that I started this process was the realization that I have damned little life outside of work anyway, the new activity rule was not very limiting. It did, however, result in the elimination of genealogy and coin collecting—on-again, off-again pursuits of mine over the years.

At the end of the day, I wound up with five possible passions to pursue and evaluate using the SCALES scale. They are:

- Sacred Harp singing
- Service club involvement
- Duplicate bridge
- Stand-up comedy
- A surprise activity at the end to keep you in suspense

I will admit that one criteria I used in coming up with this list was a desire to look at widely divergent—maybe even slightly offbeat—and relatively inexpensive activities. My hope is that if I can apply the SCALES scale to such a far-ranging group of pursuits that are not cost prohibitive, it might be suitable for you to evaluate whatever hare-brained stuff you can come up with.

Now, let the games begin.

But first, please be warned that not all issues can be explained with the SCALES scale.

> *The only cow in a small town in Texas stopped giving milk. The people did some research and found they could buy a super milk cow up in Terra Haute, Indiana, for $2,000.*
>
> *They bought the cow, and she was wonderful. She produced lots of milk every day, and people were pleased and very happy. They were so pleased*

they decided to buy a bull to mate with the cow and produce more cows like it. They would never have to worry about their milk supply again. They bought a bull and put it in the pasture with their beloved cow.

But something went wrong. Whenever the bull came close to the cow, the cow would move away. No matter what approach the bull tried, the cow would move away from the bull and he could not succeed in his quest. The people were very upset and decided to ask the town veterinarian, who was very wise, what to do.

They told the vet what was happening. "Whenever the bull approaches our cow, she moves away. If he approaches from the back, she moves forward. When he approaches her from the front, she backs off. He approaches from the side and she walks away to the other side."

The vet thought about this for a minute and asked, "Did you buy this cow in Indiana?" The people were dumbfounded, since they had never mentioned where they bought the cow. "You are truly a wise veterinarian," they said. "How did you know we got the cow in Indiana?"

The vet simply replied with a distant look in his eye, "My wife is from Indiana..."

Part II

Applying the Rules

In Search of a Passion (or Something that Flows)

10

Heading for Hayden

On the drive in to my "real job" on Tuesday morning, I realize that it is time to start thinking about the second part of this book. For months, I have been cogitating, researching, cogitating some more, and writing on the steps I need to take to find the right passion for the next leg of this long road trip, otherwise known as life. Now, the bones of that process are taking shape. Admittedly, much more work needs to be done to add meat to those bones, but the map has been drawn. So I have started asking myself, "Isn't it time to start doing some field research?"

In the back of my mind, I have always figured that Sacred Harp singing would be my first in-depth foray into post-career activities. I had first encountered the field of Sacred Harp singing about two years before. A woman, Carolyn Thompson, works as a legal assistant at my law firm and has her "space" near mine in the Birmingham offices. We exchange pleasantries each day as we go about our daily routines. One Monday, in passing, I ask her how her weekend had been. She bubbles that she had had a great weekend because she had done a weekend-long "singing." Thinking I had misheard, I stop and ask the obvious clarifying question: "What's a singing?"

Carolyn then proceeds to explain that she participates regularly in a pastime that I have never heard of—Sacred Harp singing. Sacred Harp has been a way of life for her for as long as she can remember, having been introduced to the tradition at an early age by her grandmother. She explains that once every month or so, she travels to a gathering spot, usually at a rural Alabama church, with other like-minded individuals and her well-worn hymnal, and then spends the better part of a Saturday or Sunday singing. Once or twice a month she also attends a practice singing taking place on a regular rotation at a local church. In each case, the session follows a ritual with a fairly rigid set of rules.

The established pattern calls for the "caller" at the event to call up one of the participants to stand in the "hollow square" or middle of the group, surrounded by all the other participants in all four directions. The lead singer yells out the number of the hymn that he or she wishes to sing and the verses within the hymn if less than all will be sung. At that point, one of the other participants, usually a wizened and talented older man, will act as a "keyer," or human pitch pipe, and set the key in which the song will be sung. The leader always has the option to reject the key proffered by the keyer and move the pitch up or down the musical scale, but usually relies on the keyer.

Once having decided on the key, the leader begins, and the others in the room join in, singing the first verse of the designated song in a special way. The whole group uses a unique scale comprising only four notes: fa, so, la, mi. If the extent of your knowledge of music is based on seeing Julie Andrews in her role as Fraulein Maria teach the Von Trapp children how to sing, then you know that the Sacred Harp scale is missing three notes. Sacred Harp singers overcome this shortage by repeating the first three notes as they move up the musical scale. Put another way, do-re-me-fa-sol-la-ti-do is replaced with fa-sol-la-fa-sol-la-mi-fa.

As written out in the Sacred Harp hymnal these four notes are represented by symbols that are unique to this brand of music. Sacred Harp aficionados maintain that following the written score is easier using these symbols than reading a standard music score. For obvious reasons, this musical tradition is often called "shape note" singing. The way the shapes are written (hollow, filled in, with a stick attached, with leaves on the stick) indicate the number of beats for which the note is held, much like standard musical transcription.

The alignment of singers in the room depends on the relative pitch of their voices. All members of the group are broken down into the standard designation of sopranos, altos, tenors, and basses, although Sacred Harpers refer to their sopranos as "trebles." Each of these groups has its designated line in the musical score of each hymn. That line provides the notes to be followed for each group. Each of those groups also has its assigned seating section in the room: tenors in front of the leader, trebles to the left, altos behind, and basses to the right. One variation of these seating assignments is that the first row (or two) in front of the leader is made up of the keyer and several other particularly robust singers to provide fortitude to the effort.

After the leader has run through the tune at the designated pitch, the whole Sacred Harp choir does a trial run, again using only the words fa, so, la, and mi instead of the actual words of the song. Then, having established the pitch and the tune, the entire group belts out the hymn, each singing the notes designated for their role set forth in the hymnal. All Sacred Harp authorities seem to agree that participants should stress volume and fervor over tonal accuracy—the louder the better. The leader is also charged with establishing and maintaining the beat of the song by keeping time with a chopping motion of the arm. (Think Seminole enthusiasts at a Florida State football game.) Many of the other singers will mimic this arm motion to ensure that they are on the same schedule.

After the song is finished, the leader sits down with no fanfare and to no applause. (This is a ritual, not a performance.) The caller then calls up the next leader and the process repeats itself. Usually the group doesn't quit until everyone in the room has led a song. Sometimes, the singing will go around the room multiple times, limited only by the number of hymns in the Sacred Harp hymnal. No leader is permitted to use a hymn that has already been performed at that singing.

Carolyn patiently tries to explain all of this to me. I had never heard of such a thing. Having grown up in the fairly rural South, and having sung in the church choir as a child, I was surprised to learn of such a fascinating subculture. I was intrigued, but somewhat dismissive. If I have lived this long without any knowledge of this pastime, it must enjoy a fairly small following.

My interest in this cultural phenomenon is piqued a couple of months after my discussion with Carolyn by another random conversation. I happen to be sitting next to a world-renowned marine biologist, Jim McClintock. Jim is a professor at the University of Alabama at Birmingham. His specialty is the wildlife under the ice in Antarctica. As one would suspect, most of that wildlife is fish and he knows more about those fish than anyone. He is so well known for his work in this field that the U.S. Geographic Board named a spit of land on the north side of the

McMurdo Sound in Antarctica as McClintock Point in recognition of Jim's contributions to Antarctic marine biology. On this particular day, he is the speaker at a lunch I am chairing. In my panic to make small talk with him (and since I know next to nothing about Antarctica), I mention my newfound interest in the subject of Sacred Harp singing.

He wheels around and expresses dismay. He says that his wife is a Sacred Harpist and has been looking for a group to join ever since they moved to Alabama from Southern California. I am startled to learn that a practice that I had assumed was found only in rural Alabama also has a foothold in cosmopolitan SoCal. Jim quickly accepts my offer to provide him with Carolyn's contact information.

Fast-forward a couple of months. My wife is walking to lunch in a millennial haven of Atlanta known as Virginia-Highland, when she notices a small sign outside of a neighborhood Episcopal church that reads "Sacred Harp Singing Today." Having endured my description of my personal discovery of this field, she decides to go in and hear for herself. Inside, she finds about 50 people pursuing the traditions as I had described them. She snaps and forwards some photos to me to prove that Sacred Harp is alive and well in the inner city of Atlanta.

On its face, none of this makes any sense. If you have a hankering to sing hymns, most churches have organized choirs and you can exercise your vocal chords each week with your fellow parishioners. I have to wonder what causes folks to travel not insignificant distances to meet up with others, many of whom are total strangers, to sing the same songs over and over. Clearly, to fully understand the draw of Sacred Harp singing, to discover all of the facets of the traditions, and to determine whether it might be a suitable long-term passion would require actual participation. Sometime. In the future.

Carolyn had given me a schedule of singing a few months back. But I wasn't ready. I was working on Part 1 of this book and trying to set some parameters for what and how to write Part 2. I had the best of intentions of exploring Sacred Harp singing after I settled on the criteria I should use to evaluate it.

At least that is how I am thinking on this Tuesday in early October—I'll get an updated schedule and think about attending a singing "sometime," maybe after the first of the year. When I ask her for a new schedule, she says: "Oh, the County Line singing's taking place this weekend. It's a great one, some of the best food ever, and it's not too far from here. You should come." Gulp! Goodbye, comfort zone. I thank her and tell her I will think about it.

After going into my office and thinking about my conversation, I have to give myself a talking to. If I am serious about this process, there are no good excuses not to go. The location is proximate, the event is representative, and the date it turned out was especially convenient as my wife would be out of town on babysitting duty in Atlanta with our grandchild. Oh, hell...out of convenient excuses.

The next day I accept Carolyn's invitation and ask for directions to the County Line singing scheduled for the following Sunday. She writes out the directions and tells me some of the rules: Starting time, 9:30. Must stay for lunch as this event is known for its good cooks, and the singing improves with full bellies. Don't bring food as I will be a guest and the hosts would be offended if a visitor brings food. Expect to be introduced. Expect to be required to stand in the hollow square for maximum effect.

On Saturday night, I pull out the directions that Caroline had provided and determine that her estimate of a 30-minute travel time was at least 15 minutes shy of the real time it will take me to get to the singing. The location was pegged at some 7 miles off Interstate 65 as you head north toward Huntsville. The nearest town of any size is Hayden, Alabama, and it barely warrants mention on the sign for Exit 284. I decide to allot myself a full hour to get there.

On Sunday morning, I leave the house at 8:15 for the 9:30 singing. After 30 minutes, I am making such good time that I reward myself by stopping at the McDonald's in Gardendale, Alabama, for a sausage biscuit and some great people watching. Then, I climb in my car for the short culmination of the trip. That's when I realize that the printed directions for the singing are sitting on the kitchen island back at my house. At this point, driving back for the directions would cause me to be at least an hour late—an auspicious start to my venture. I might as well go home and try again another day.

Time for another internal personal confrontation. Had I just had a brain cramp and forgotten the directions or was this a subliminal attempt to keep me squarely inside my comfort zone. In either event, returning home is not a suitable option. I recall from the night before that the first step in the directions is to take Exit 284 (Hayden/Corner) and then turn back under the interstate. I launch off for the aforementioned exit hoping that the rest of the turns would be self-evident. No such luck. A hundred yards after passing under the highway, I dead-end into a highway with no relevant signage, and no idea which way to turn nor how far to go.

I check to see if I have a cell number for Carolyn. No luck. A Google search for "County Line Sacred Harp Singing" produces no results. Likewise for "Sacred Harp Singing Hayden." The more generic search term "Sacred Harp Singing Alabama" produces the sought-for result, some telephone numbers affiliated with a singing on this day.

The first number has been disconnected. The second number references an Emily Creel Brown and I remember that Carolyn had mentioned that the singing was sponsored by the Creel family. I dial the number with little hope of success as I am now within 10 minutes of the scheduled start time. After several rings, a tentative voice answers. After being reassured that I am not a pollster or solicitor, Emily brightens, offers encouragement and assures me that I don't have far to go to reach the singing.

The next several miles of driving take me farther and farther off the beaten path. I pass a string of modest homes and small farms. Virtually every other house has a "Trump—Make America Great" sign in the yard and no signs of support for the former Secretary of State. I pass from Jefferson County into Blount County, and then back into Jefferson County (thus, the moniker "County Line"), and then turn onto Miller Road, which soon becomes a gravel road. Shortly, I come to what appears to be a small country church: a white cinderblock-and-clapboard building with a high-pitched roof. In the yard outside the building are about a dozen cars and pickup trucks with about that many again lining the road. I park and walk inside just after 9:30 a.m.

The singing has just started. In the main room are 25 people sitting in pews and a few folding chairs behind the leader, singing with gusto as the leader keeps the beat with the chop motion. I immediately spot Carolyn sitting in the second pew. She expresses surprise that I have actually made the trek, but she has saved me a seat and she hands me a hymnal. I am thrust into my first Sacred Harp singing without any opportunity to calmly adjust to my new environment.

For the next hour, we sing song after song, as a parade of singers are called to the front to declare a hymn number and mouth the tune. Then the rest of the room picks up the song and carries on. I do my best to sing along, following the bass line in the musical score. For me, this is really tough. My trouble is caused by a combination of being very rusty in my music reading (the St. James choir is 45 years in my past) and the unique musical notation used in a Sacred Harp hymnal.

I soon come to realize, it doesn't matter. The other basses in the room drown out my many mistakes, and nobody really cares anyway. They seem to be caught up in the pure enjoyment of belting out a familiar (to them) tune. If I'm off-key, it just gives them more reason to turn up their own volume.

By the time we reach the first "12-minute break," the size of the crowd has more than doubled to about 65. I am now able to take a breath, look around the room, and drink in my surroundings. The room is large enough that it could easily accommodate another 50 or so people. There is no altar per se, but there is a table a few feet behind the hollow square that has a simple flower arrangement upon it and a cross that sits slightly above eye level. Other than that, the room is unadorned. The participants in the room are all white, with slightly more women than men. In attendance are people of all ages, from babes in arms to older men and women using walkers, but most of the participants are over the age of 50 and most of the younger people seem to be Creel relatives.

As it turns out, the Creel family has been hosting singings in this area since 1919. The building, a former church, is owned by an out-of-state family, but the owners have allowed it to be used solely for singings "forever." Members of the Creel family maintain the old church as a matter of pride and tradition. For the past several decades, it has been used only for the two singings a year—one in October and one in April—but there are plans to attract other singing groups to the area. The April singing is held in conjunction with the "decorating" of the family cemetery, which is another 50 yards down the road. At the April event, after the singing, the family proceeds to the cemetery and places flowers on the graves in memory of the dearly departed. Of the people in the room, 25 or so seem to be members of the family, although their last names are now Brown, Jett, Ellis, Capps, and King (as well as Creel).

After the break, the singing resumes. The original keyer is replaced by another, younger man. (Carolyn says there is a conscious effort underway to bring on the next generation of keyers as many of the experienced ones are "dying out." In fact, she says there is a trend of younger singers keying their own songs.) Occasionally, a new leader will throw out a hymn number and be shouted down on the grounds that the song has already been sung.

Soon, Carolyn's name is called and she rises and grabs me by the arm to move to the square. She introduces me to the group, saying that I work in the law firm with her and that I am known in the office as the White House Man. (This is not a nickname I have ever heard before, and I presume it refers to my having worked in Washington, D.C. in years past.) She then calls the number of her preferred hymn and mouths the tune. At this point, I get to experience the audio sensation of standing in the midst of an a cappella chorus of spiritual music blasted from all directions by 65 enthusiastic voices. Some of the emotional impact on me is deflected because I am struggling to sing the appointed tune without embarrassing myself. Nevertheless, it is a uniquely moving experience.

We finish our song and return to our seats. The process continues until I notice that several of the participants, mostly women, are taking their leave of the main room and drifting through the doors behind the cross into another room. Soon, it becomes apparent that they have gone to put out the dishes they have lovingly brought for lunch as a halt is called to the singing and we move into the other room for lunch.

When I make my way into the adjacent room, I find a feast has been set out. On folding tables in the middle of the room are no fewer than 25 main dishes, ranging from fried chicken, meatloaf, and Conecuh County sausage to a wide variety of vegetables. On another table set against the wall are about 10 scrumptious dessert dishes. Not wanting to insult any of the cooks, I take small helpings of as many dishes as I can fit on my plate. Carolyn was correct. This is no place to bring a diet. The food at the County Line singing deserves its reputation for good down-home cooking (especially the pecan pie).

Before and during lunch, I make it a point to circulate around the room and get a feel for the people who have come to take part in this event. I meet Buell Cobb from Vestavia Hills. Jim Carns from Montgomery works with Alabama Arise, a community organizing group focused on social issues. Brett King is a lawyer from Locust Fork. His wife knows Lucy Bynum, wife of my law partner Stanley. I run into Don Ellis, whom I used to know in the mortgage business. As is so often the case in the South, there are only a couple of degrees of separation between many of the attendees and me. Once again I am struck by the fact that until a few months ago I had nary an inkling that this pastime even existed.

Many of the misconceptions I held about the group are dispelled. My assumption that I would be attending a church service, albeit with a heavy emphasis on the choral elements, was incorrect. While there is a clear Christian overtone to the proceedings, including the cross on the table, a general prayer of Thanksgiving and inspiration early, an invocation before lunch, and Judeo-Christian lyrics to all of the hymns, there is no preaching or proselytizing. Carolyn says that several of the singers are Jewish (and maybe even a Muslim somewhere, although that statement is pretty indefinite) and that all faiths (and even nonbelievers) are welcome. Moreover, there really doesn't seem to be any real motivation behind the attendance of the folks I visit with other than pure enjoyment. They have gotten to know each other over the years, and they like singing. There is no question that the event is far and away more about the singing and socializing than the praying.

I can't help but contrast my experience here with the 9:00 Sunday service at my Episcopal church in Birmingham. There, the organ and choir are the primary sources of musical sounds, and most congregants just listen in. When it comes time for a hymn, most non-choir members seem to only mouth the words, at best. In the longtime traditions of the holy and apostolic church, you get participation in the form of the prayers that are recited in silent contemplation or in unison with the priest, more prayers than that recited for you, a sermon, and a sacrament, but the average member is more an observer of the music from the stands than a member of the starting team. Not so at County Line. Everyone here is expected on the field for every play.

The Sacred Harp participants also do not fit the stereotype I had conjured up in my mind in the days before the singing. I had assumed, incorrectly, that all of the attendees would be locals who had little else to do on a Sunday in rural Alabama. Instead, I meet lawyers, retired mortgage bankers, schoolteachers, and conservationists. Some of the folks in the room, particularly members of the Creel family, are from the nearby area, but there are also folks from Montgomery and Huntsville. I even meet one man who has come all the way from Nebraska. It turns out that the County Line singing is somewhat famous in Sacred Harp circles.

Finally, I am blown away by how hospitable the group is. Many of the regulars go out of their way to introduce themselves, and everyone I meet goes to great lengths to make me feel welcome. And the food—the food is fabulous. It reminds me of potluck meals in my youth where each cook, as a matter of pride, would choose dishes that had been proven through many similar occasions to be crowd-pleasers. Carolyn warned me to expect to overeat, but she had not fully set the mental table for me. Clearly, singings are not good places to pursue a personal weight loss program.

The singing breaks up about 2:30, and everybody makes their way to their cars, after reminders that the next County Line singing will take place on the second Sunday in April. The group disperses with the usual promises to stay in touch and get together at the next singing on the calendar. The "church" is cleaned up and closed up until the Creel family gathers with their Sacred Harp friends in the spring to sing and decorate the family graves.

On my way back home I ponder what I have just experienced. The group that I have spent the better part of my Sunday with was well organized, dedicated, and just as passionate about their pursuit as any golfer or college football tailgater. They were absorbed in the singing, all the while enjoying the interaction with the other singers. During breaks and at lunch, they were surrounded by friends and family and enjoying each other's company independent of, but enhanced by, the common experience that comes along with the singing of the hymns. Given that many of the ingredients of the SCALES scale seemed to be present, I determine that more research is in order.

That research starts with a couple of simple questions: What the hell is Sacred Harp singing, and where did it come from? The tradition, it turns out, traces its roots back to "country parish music" of early 18th-century England. Choral musicians found that using a simple musical notation where each note was represented on a musical score by a different shape made it easier for congregants, many of whom were illiterate, to join in the singing of hymns without the need for musical accompaniment.

At some point in the mid-1700s, these simple techniques traveled with immigrants to the New World, and many small Protestant congregations in New England adopted similar a cappella methods due to the ease of assimilation and the simplicity of shape note musical notation. Over time, the techniques grew into disfavor in the Northeast as the churches grew and the congregations adopted more "sophisticated" music influenced by European churches and accompanied by organs and pianos.

The shaped note, a cappella style hung on, however, in the more rural areas, particularly in the South. In 1844, Sacred Harp as a formal variety of shaped note music was born with the publication of *The Sacred Harp* by B. F. White and E. J. King,[97] two musicians from rural Georgia. (Adherents often state categorically that the term "sacred harp" is a metaphor for the human voice, but it is not clear that White and King believed that.) For decades thereafter, the tradition saw a surge in popularity with the growth of revivals in the South.

From the mid-1800s to the early 20th century, Sacred Harp singing has maintained a small but determined following in the Southern United States and particularly in the rural areas of the Deep South. As with any tradition of this type, there have been several schisms among its practitioners as some groups have tried to modernize the hymns, while others maintain strict adherence to the traditions and music set forth by the early composers.

The 1970s saw a resurgence in the popularity of Sacred Harp singing, and it began to spread outside of the rural South. In 1985, the first Illinois convention was held in recognition of the support that the tradition was receiving in the Chicago area. Now, there are groups regularly conducting singings throughout the United States, including most urban areas, and in several foreign countries. Even in its present form, you would be hard-pressed to describe Sacred Harp singing as ubiquitous, but it has a widely dispersed and diverse following.

With this background in mind, I return to my original quest. My initiation into Sacred Harp at the County Line singing and learning more of the history of the tradition has piqued my curiosity. I decide that I need to delve deeper to see how this lifestyle would rank on the SCALES scale. In preparation for my next singing, I determine that I need to learn how to do it correctly. After all, this shaped note stuff is supposed to make singing easy for the rest of us, right? I locate an instruction book on Sacred Harp music and start educating myself. I quickly learn that it is not as easy as they try to make it sound.

Step one is to learn the shapes. That is pretty easy: "fa" is a triangle, "sol" is an oval, "la" is a rectangle, and "mi" is a diamond. Each represents a note on a typical musical scale, as illustrated in standard fashion.[98]

Fa Sol La Fa Sol La Mi Fa

1 2 3 4 5 6 7 8

F major scale

Then you have different colorations of the shapes to indicate relative length of the note. An empty shape is a whole note. If it is empty but has a stick stuck to it, it is a half note. If it has a stick coming off of it and it is colored in, it is a quarter note. A stick with leaves coming off the shape is an eighth note. Here is what all of these look like.[99]

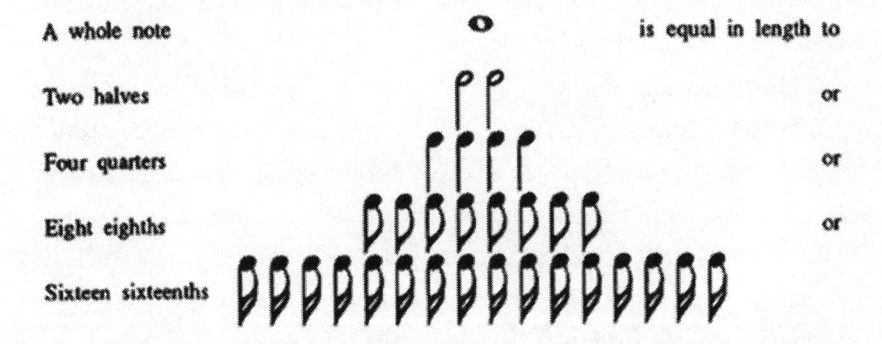

A whole note   o   is equal in length to

Two halves   or

Four quarters   or

Eight eighths   or

Sixteen sixteenths

In the Sacred Harp hymnal, the notes are arranged on a musical score consisting of four lines, one line each for each section of the room: trebles, altos, tenors, and basses—with the assigned notes for each ranging from highest pitch to lowest for each tune. So far, so good. Some of this reminds me of singing in the choir as a boy, and I can relate to the concepts.

Then this shaped note stuff starts to get confusing. The material goes into major scales and minor scales, and refers to treble clefts and bass clefts. The book then introduces the concept of "intervals" and "steps" and I am totally lost. I run to Carolyn for advice, and she is quick to calm me down and tell me that I am making it way too complicated. I just need to go to more singings, listen to some recordings while following along with a hymnal, and enjoy the music. Stated another way—my words, not hers—I need to leave my Type A-need-to-know-everything-at-once approach at the door and savor the experience.

Carolyn also offers up a couple of websites that have video recordings of Sacred Harp groups singing songs from the hymnal. I make plans to attend the annual Alabama Sacred Harp Convention singing on the weekend after Thanksgiving, and I make a commitment to spend some time beforehand following (and singing) along with as many of the video offerings as possible. Having been talked down off the ledge, I figure I can do this.

The written material on Sacred Harp singing makes a point of stating that as a general rule volume trumps accuracy—at a singing, it is better to sing loud than to hit the precise note shown in the hymnal. I also quickly discover, upon the advice of my sweet wife, that singing practice by an individual who has limited ability to read music is best done out of the earshot of others, including the earshot of your sweet wife. Thus, banished to the basement and other lonesome confines, I practice many of the songs, earbuds in, volume up.

It is hard. Most of the tunes are unfamiliar to me, and most of the melodies that I do recognize have new words. Occasionally, I can find a rendering of an old standby, such as "Amazing Grace" (a.k.a. "New Britain"),[100] but I still struggle trying to read the bass line of the music. I am completely bumfuzzled by the first round of every song when the group goes through the melody one time using fa-sol-la-mi's in place of the words. I know how the shape of the notes are meant to correspond with the corresponding syllable, but it is a struggle to spit them out at the proper tone and speed in unison with the singers on the videos. In short, this is hard work.

Over the course of several sessions, however, it gets slightly less hard. In part, because I learn a few tricks. If it is a new tune, you can fake the fasola round by just using "la." Also, some of the more popular tunes are really infectious. In fact, I find myself humming some of the favorites the day after my last session. While not becoming second nature by a long shot, it is also becoming slightly easier to follow the musical notation in the hymnal. As my next in-person singing approaches, I feel much more prepared to attend as a knowledgeable, albeit not very seasoned, participant.

On the Saturday after Thanksgiving, my wife, my grown daughter, my 14-month-old grandson, and I launch off on an adventure—attendance at the annual gathering of the Alabama State Sacred Harp Convention and Singing held this year at Jefferson State Community College near Centerpoint, Alabama. After a 45-minute sojourn through the winding back roads of north Jefferson County, we arrive at the campus. We are able to find the Fitzgerald Activity Center fairly easily because it is the only building on this bleak weekend morning with cars parked in front of it. Moreover, the only people we see entering the nondescript building are toting hymnals. It doesn't take much deductive reasoning to conclude that we are in the right place.

Inside, there are about a hundred people milling about. Most seem to know one another, and many greet each other like old friends at a reunion. In the registration hallway, a few tables have been set up to allow the more entrepreneurial singers to hawk CDs and DVDs they have recorded at singings, or books they have written on the subject. The blandness of the building is repeated inside, and that theme continues as we are called into the room where the singing will take place. This room is filled with folding chairs, some of which have been arranged in a "Sacred Harp square" so that tenors face altos, trebles face basses, and there is a hollow square in the middle.

In short order, the group divides itself into the seats corresponding to their voices and the fasola verse of the first song is sung. I had missed the beginning of the singing in Hayden, so I didn't realize that the tradition in this community is to use the first song as the lead-up to an opening prayer. As the song concludes, an appointed member of the group gives a brief invocation of divine provenance and offering of thanks, the assembled group sits, and the singing commences in earnest.

The overall operation is very efficient, with a group of organizers sitting at an elevated table in the front left corner of the room. As each song ends, one of these organizers calls up a leader and announces who is on deck to lead the next song. As in Hayden, the leader calls out the number of the song to be sung as he or she approaches the hollow square. The pitch is offered by the keyer, the tune is sung by the whole group using only fa-so-la-mi words, and then the hymn is sung. If the hymnal shows more than two verses, the accepted practice seems to be that only the first and last verses are sung. The leader walks back to his or her seat, while the new leader approaches the square and the process repeats. In the space of an hour, the group belts out a dozen songs.

During the first couple of hours of the singing, I learn a couple of lessons. First, the rule of "louder beats accurate" is alive and well at the annual meeting of the Alabama Convention. In fact, one slightly off-key Mennonite soprano in the first row easily, but not pleasantly, is able to drown out a whole bass section.

My other revelation is that singings are not the best place to take toddlers. My grandson is only temporarily impressed by the singing and then wants to explore other attractions and venues. My daughter and wife take turns trying to provide the necessary diversions, but they are becoming less and less enamored with their decision to join me and others are beginning to become annoyed with the distraction. The combination of lessons one and two is that my second singing is abbreviated and we leave at the first break, after purchasing some DVDs to help me prepare better for the next singing.

After the singing at Jeff State, I renew my efforts to hone my skills as a Sacred Harp singer. The DVDs help a little by giving me some of the background of shaped note traditions. Of more help are the YouTube segments of actual singings around the country. These allow me to sing along in the privacy of my own home. (Let me stress the privacy part. I may not be quick to become a polished singer, but my realization that no one wants to be in the room while I am learning is almost immediate.) After hours and hours of practice over the succeeding several weeks, I believe I am improving (and since there is no one else around to contradict me, it must be true) and I am ready to try another singing. I talk to Carolyn and we decide that my next exposure to a group should be at a singing coming up in Tuscaloosa at the Canterbury Episcopal Chapel on the campus of the University of Alabama.

My primary motivation behind picking this particular singing is hopefully to catch a glimpse of the next generation of singers. My logic is that the location is convenient to tens of thousands of college students and any who are musically inclined might be attracted to this a cappella singing opportunity. Even those without musical talents (like me) might be curious and attend to witness a wonderful cultural tradition. Such youthful participation could provide insight regarding the future for Sacred Harp singing. Sadly, I was mistaken.

Of the 50 or so attendees, only two or three appeared to be college students. Of those, one confessed to being from rural Alabama and it turned out that she was accompanying her grandfather. The others showed up just to observe after the mid-morning break and seemed to be more interested in the abundant home-cooked lunch offerings than the singing. A possible explanation for the lack of visitors from the University was the plethora of pregame diversions around campus due to a soon-to-occur tip-off of an SEC basketball game involving the Alabama Crimson Tide. (The same pending athletic event also caused the singing to conclude an hour early.) Whether or not there is a NextGen future for Sacred Harp, one of my important takeaways is this: Don't ever, ever try to compete with SEC athletics!

The absence of college students at this singing also portends another reality in the world of Sacred Harp singing. Clearly, the faithful are aging. As I looked around the room in Tuscaloosa, I noticed several of the attendees needed to rely on canes to maintain their maneuverability. One older lady sat in a wheelchair with an oxygen tank and just listened. As I talked to the folks around me, I learned almost all were retirees. I made a point of approaching some of the younger singers and discovered that most of them had come from other parts of Alabama, usually rural areas, and had been raised in the Sacred Harp traditions from tender ages. The recent recruits to the practice whom I found were generally older and had had some other background in music. In addition, it seemed that every third or fourth song was dedicated to a former Sacred Harp singer who had recently met his or her maker. When added together, my assessment for the longevity of the pastime is not rosy.

Nevertheless, the singing is a delightful gathering composed of an interesting group of people. By the end of the event, all of those who wanted to lead a hymn got their chance—twice. The location, the parish hall of the church, is cozy but comfortable for the size of the assembled group. The leaders and keyers are enthusiastic and talented. The food, as rumored, is delicious and abundant. I recognize several of the participants from the County Line and Alabama Convention singings. In fact, I found that I can comfortably continue prior conversations from prior singings in a couple of cases.

Perhaps the most interesting conversation of the day is with Tom Booth, a retired nurse from Cullman, a fairly small city in north-central Alabama. It turns out that Tom had retired to Cullman in the last couple of years from his career in Fresno, California. He had chosen Cullman for two reasons. First, the state and local tax codes are kinder and gentler to retirees in Alabama than those in California. But second, and more importantly according to Tom, the Sacred Harp singing group needed him. He had attended a singing there several years ago, and the local leader of the group had implored him to set up permanent residence in the area and join the group. It had taken Tom four years to convince his wife that moving to Cullman was the right decision. She is now an avid singer as well, and they are both tickled with their relocation. Given the Booths' experience, perhaps the Alabama visitors bureau needs to rethink its ad campaigns and focus on California and the Sacred Harp opportunities in my state.

While the day at the singing in Tuscaloosa is enjoyable and interesting, it is also painfully revealing. My skills in reading the music laid out in the Sacred Harp hymnal and rendering the melodies it portrays have not measurably improved. Others in the room are hospitable and careful not to embarrass me. (Although, the lady in the wheelchair occasionally furrows her brow and scowls at me when I stray from the desired notes.) At some point, it becomes necessary to wake up and smell the Conecuh sausage—singing takes talent, and I ain't got it.

Having reached the conclusion that I am not naturally predisposed to be a Sacred Harp singer, I think it only fair to give the tradition a reasoned assessment on all fronts. In other words, how does Sacred Harp singing rate on the SCALES scale as a possible passion to pursue? I may not be good at it, but does it rate with all of the elements that increase the odds that I will live a longer, more content life? Here's my play-by-play, postgame analysis:

Social interaction—I give Sacred Harp a high ranking for this factor. The singings are not just a group performance. The regular breaks and the emphasis placed on the long, leisurely (and gluttonous) mid-session meals at most gatherings illustrate the purely social aspects of the singings. It would be easy to portray the episodic nature of the singings as too sporadic to offer much in the way of social support, but that is not my impression. For newcomers, as I have been, everyone bends over backwards to be cordial and hospitable. Moreover, the singers seem to develop friendships over time that transcend the vocal activities. The best illustration of those relationships is the time devoted at each meeting to making the group aware of the sick and shut-in amongst the ranks, along with encouragement to reach out and offer assistance. (In addition, many leaders dedicate their songs to those who have passed on to their eternal rewards.)

Plus, there seems to be a good deal of communication among participants throughout the periods between organized singings. Some of this is the natural result of the relationships that have been forged over years of traveling to, and participating in, far-flung songfests. Also, a good deal of organizational activities have to take place to plan for and pull off a gathering of dozens of folks, many of whom are from out of the area. Clearly, the participants bond in ways that transcend simple participation in a musical event.

Nevertheless, for me, the social interaction that comes with the pursuit seems to be intermittent, at best. Even if I had been more regular, I would have been usually singing only on weekends with an occasional practice session during the week. Because the locations of the events are spread out, both geographically and temporally, my social interactions would be hard to describe as broad and frequent. As a result, I assign a score of 7 for this element.

Concentration, in the form of brain stimulation—Although billed as a form of music that is intended for everyone, clearly I don't fit into that category. For me, Sacred Harp singing is like trying to learn a foreign language. As such, each song is a struggle made only somewhat easier with the knowledge that my responsibility is volume not precision.

I suspect that, like a foreign language, over time, reading the music would become second nature, including being able to read along with the fa-so-la chorus. And once all of the tunes become familiar, reading the music would become more of a reminder than a guidepost. In fact, some of the tunes have already started to pop into my head at weird times, long after the singing is over. The begrudging familiarity I have gained, however, is vastly overshadowed by the ongoing struggle to master this new language.

Admittedly, this rating exercise is very subjective, but I am the subject in this subjective process, and my encounter with the world of Sacred Harpists has caused me to accept a painful truth—music is not in my inherent skill set. I understand the theory, but trying to read shaped notes and simultaneously cause my voice box to emit the sound that corresponds to those notes is very difficult, requiring intense concentration (and constant frustration). I just don't seem to have the knack for this pastime.

When I mention my apparent lack of the necessary musical talents to Carolyn Thompson, who ushered me into this world to start with, she says: "It takes every bit of four years to get the hang of it, but it's a whole lot of fun along the way." Perhaps, but it is the challenge that counts here, and I have to declare Sacred Harp singing as pretty intense in the concentration category and assign it a score of 9 on this front.

Accomplishment, in the form of setting and striving for a goal or a result— As far as I can tell, there are few discernible goals associated with Sacred Harp. Perhaps, for some, there is an overarching goal of sustaining a pastime that has been important to generations of their family—the Creel family comes to mind. I suppose it is a minor miracle, and thus an accomplishment, that a room of 100 participants can engage in an activity that allows each of those in attendance to perform, more or less on an equal basis, with everyone else. I also suppose that you could create a goal for your involvement, such as attending every singing in a state in a given year. But for me, I never felt a feeling of accomplishment. As a result, I assign a score of 2 on this element.

Laughter, in the form of fun and enjoyment—By and large, singers seem to be a pretty serious bunch. Certainly not many guffaws while the hymnals were open. Occasionally, during breaks or before the music started, I might witness a small group enjoying a private joke—emphasis on occasionally. But I recognize that for many others not all enjoyment involves laughter.

Clearly, the group of regulars who travel, often long distances, to participate in organized singings enjoy the experience. The enthusiasm is there, and the smiles are on their faces (in most cases), even if there is a dearth of chortling.

That having been said, once again I come back to the reality that this is a subjective enterprise, and I had trouble finding the fun in this pastime. In fact, I can't remember any instance of my laughing out loud at any point during my involvement with the singings. (In hindsight, it could be that I was the joke.) As a result, I have to give Sacred Harp a low score of 2 in this category.

Exercise, in the form of some physical exertion—If, as my research indicates, laughter is a form of exercise, there must be some physical benefits that accrue from singing as well. It only follows that belting out "Amazing Grace" at the top of your lungs—not to mention the Cherokee chop method of keeping time with the music—must earn you some physical fitness points, right? If so, the scientific world is slow to recognize them. A quick Internet search for the health benefits of Sacred Harp singing produces nada. Even a search for the physical benefits of singing generally produces only a few studies indicating that the deep breathing that comes along with singing may generate some worthwhile results from a respiratory and cardiac perspective. Let's just say that sitting in a chair, singing along, and keeping time is not the same as a cardio workout at the gym. This ain't HIIT. I assign a score of 2 for exercise.

Spirituality—No question that the lyrics of the hymns carry a fundamental Christian message. In fact, it is easy to find verses in the Sacred Harp hymnal that fit comfortably into the concepts of overall wellness described by doctors Ryff and Seligman. Consider the words of the first verse of hymn 98:[101]

> Why should we at our lot complain
> Or grieve at our distress?
> Some think if they could riches gain
> They'd gain true happiness.
> Ah! We're much to blame.
> We're all the same—
> Alike we're made of clay;
> Then, since we have a Savior dear,
> Let's drive all care away.

I found it difficult to tell, however, whether many of the singers were paying attention to the words of the songs. Of course, there was an invocation of the blessings of a Judeo-Christian God at each gathering and many prayers offered up to the memory of the dearly departed. As with just about any activity, the level of spirituality is what you want it to be, and Sacred Harp certainly provides abundant opportunity for a participant to look inward. As discussed in the chapter on spirituality, each to his own.

At the Tuscaloosa singing, while sitting under a tree outside and gorging myself on the wonderful lunch, I had a conversation with one of the few younger people in the group of attendees, Elizabeth Gentry. Elizabeth is in her mid-30s, and originally had plans to be a medical missionary to further her beliefs as a member of the Church of Christ. While on a mission trip to Africa, she decided that she was not cut out for mission work as a full-time pursuit. She went back to Auburn University to study engineering and now works for UPS. But she also recently accepted the volunteer position as the vice-chair of the Auburn Sacred Harp group.

When I asked Elizabeth if this form of singing was a spiritual pursuit for her, she was quick to answer in the affirmative. She said that she feels closer to God when she sings and that the words of many of the hymns hold special meaning to her in a prayerful way. She also opined that the ability to sing, in her view, is a gift from God. (Had she been sitting near me in the bass section, she might have qualified this last statement.) Clearly, for Elizabeth, Sacred Harp singing has a host of spiritual qualities.

From my own standpoint, spirituality in any of my Sacred Harp sessions was lacking. I probably spent too much time focused on trying to read the music and veer my voice toward the proper notes and not enough time on the message. While each singing had prayers recited at intervals throughout the day (e.g., an opening invocation, in memory of a recent death, a blessing for the midday meal), they seemed somewhat perfunctory to me. Some in the crowd, like Elizabeth, seemed to know the tunes and words by heart, and may have been in a more spiritual place, but I never got there. I was too busy trying to sing without embarrassing myself. As a result, I never felt that I had an experience that passed for spirituality, or even that would get me a get-out-of-church-free card. Nevertheless, I view this as a shortcoming of mine rather than a lacking owing to Sacred Harp. Accordingly, I give Sacred Harp an 8 on the spirituality scale.

When you put all of these scores into my handy-dandy matrix, you come to a score of 5.6 on the SCALES scale. As this is the first activity ever to be so scored in the history of mankind, it is difficult to assess how this result ranks in my world of possible post-retirement activities. It is worth noting, however, that if the state of flow as promised by Mihaly Csikszentmihalyi is one of the indicators that you are succeeding in the pursuit of happiness, Sacred Harp singing doesn't appear to hold much promise for me. I never looked up and said "Wow, look at the clock; where did the day go?" Nor did I feel that my natural talents were kicking in to contribute toward the accomplishment of a worthwhile purpose. The whole exercise has been mildly entertaining and vastly informative, but the mystical state of flow seems elusive in my Sacred Harp world.

When all is said and done, though, hanging out with friends at a singing is much less tricky at my age than trying the bar scene.

> *A gentleman in his mid-nineties, very well dressed, hair well groomed, great-looking suit, flower in his lapel, smelling slightly of a good aftershave, walks into an upscale cocktail lounge.*
>
> *Seated at the bar is an attractive, slightly younger lady, in her mid-eighties.*
>
> *The gentleman walks over, sits alongside her, orders a drink, turns to her, and says, "So tell me, do I come here often?"*

11

Heading for Harbert

I'm sitting in my office one day in September in 2013, minding my own business, and I get a call from an old friend, Charlie Perry. He wants to have breakfast. I am always up for a meal, so I immediately agree, but my internal warning sirens have activated. Charlie is not only a friend but also a community activist. Not in the carrying signs and pulling down statues sense, but in the active-in-community-service sense. He has served on the boards of various worthwhile civic endeavors and has been known to pass the hat to raise money for his favorite eleemosynary causes. I enjoy Charlie's company, but we are not close enough that he would want to go grab a bite to shoot the shit and talk college football. My mind immediately jumps to the conclusion that this meal is going to cost a lot more than the price of an omelet.

When I arrive at 7:30 a.m. at the Over Easy Restaurant, waiting for me are not only Charlie but several other friends—all of them community activists. This is a bad development for my prospects of avoiding being tapped for whatever capital campaign is at issue. And then it dawns on me—the thread that runs throughout this group is that each of them, at one time or another, has been the president of the Rotary Club of Birmingham.

In the Birmingham area, there are several Rotary clubs. The oldest and largest is the one that meets at a downtown location for lunch almost every Wednesday—the Rotary Club of Birmingham, a.k.a. the Downtown Rotary. For the last decade or so, the Downtown Rotary has vied each year for the title of Largest Rotary Club in the World, and it is always in the top two or three as measured by the number of members on its rolls.

Once the unifying characteristic of my breakfast group occurs to me, I come to suspect the purpose of the meeting. This group represents the nominating committee of the Downtown Rotary, and they are looking for a nominee for the position of president-elect. After being offered the position, I indicate my appreciation for the (misguided) confidence their offer implies, but request a little time to consider the role and to explore whether my "day job" would allow for the time commitment that serving as president would require. About a week later, I call Charlie and accept the offer. Thus begins a two-year deep dive into the world of service clubs.

Service clubs have been around in the United States in one form or another for centuries. When Alexis de Tocqueville penned *Democracy in America*,[102] based on his tour of America in the early 1830s, he drew attention to the degree to which Americans formed groups to serve personal interests and solve both large and small problems. Over the years, such organizations have taken a number of forms and maintained unique causes and profiles, including the Freemasons, the Elks Club, the Optimists, the League of Women Voters, the Shriners, the Sierra Club, and the Junior League. Some are affiliated with certain religious denominations, such as the Knights of Columbus. In other cases, membership may be grounded in military service as with the Veterans of Foreign Wars.

Membership in these organizations has waxed and waned over the years, but generally reached its apex in the 1950s. According to the Corporation for National Community Service, volunteerism in the United States as defined broadly as involvement with school, civic, religious, and other service organizations has been on the decline for well over a decade.[103] In his widely regarded 1993 study of civic engagement in the United States, Robert Putnam noted that the trends toward less organized social and political activity started in the Sixties.[104] Without question, service and civic clubs have not been immune to the general societal trends toward more individualism and less organized activities.

My experience, though, has shown that it is a little too early to start writing the obituaries for the larger and more active service clubs. For purposes of this discussion, I define "service club" fairly narrowly as a voluntary nonprofit organization where members meet regularly to perform charitable works either by direct hands-on efforts or by raising money for donation to those causes. As so defined, service comes first, but there is also an element of social interaction, networking, and personal growth and improvement as a result of the regular face-to-face meetings.

The largest service clubs today, in order of total membership, are the Lions Club International, Rotary International, and Kiwanis International. As the formal names would imply, each is international in scope. Membership in these clubs is not limited by gender, ethnicity, or religious affiliation. Each also has a formal mission that incorporates service, and each has an overarching charitable focus. Lions focus on eyesight issues. Rotarians have been working on the global eradication of polio for decades. Kiwanians pay particular attention to children's issues. The work of each organization extends beyond their stated causes, but they use the big central issue as a rallying cry.

Birmingham, Alabama, and more specifically the Harbert Center in the heart of downtown Birmingham, is a somewhat unique epicenter in the service club universe. Two of the three largest international organizations, Rotary and Kiwanis, have one of their largest local chapters housed in the same building on 4th Avenue North—the Harbert Center. The building was constructed in 1992, when two civic leaders, John Harbert and Hall Thompson, recognized the need for permanent meeting and office facilities for the two clubs and that such a place could also serve as a suitable meeting space for a variety of community groups and social activities. It is this world into which I plunged after accepting the invitation to join the leadership ladder of the Downtown Rotary.

In all honesty, I originally had joined the Rotary somewhat reluctantly in the mid-1990s. After I took a new job as an officer of a regional mortgage company based in Birmingham, my new boss encouraged me to sign up as a way to become more involved in the local community. I followed his advice, although my travel schedule caused me frequently to miss the weekly meetings. I was vaguely aware that the motto of Rotary International is "Service Above Self," but I used my busy work schedule and responsibilities at home helping to raise two young daughters as excuses not to volunteer for any of the community service opportunities proffered by the group. You might say that I was not in the running to be Rotarian of the Year, any year.

My profile in the Downtown Rotary started to change in 2009. In that year, the incoming club president, Charlie Perry (the same one who, years later, would ask me to breakfast), called to see if I would be willing to help him by serving as the head of his Program Committee. The Program Committee is the group charged with the task of lining up the weekly speakers for the meetings. I had just returned to town after my three-year stint in Washington, D.C., and Charlie hoped that my time in our Nation's Capital would give me a window on a previously untapped slate of speakers who would be appealing to our membership and who could speak on previously uncovered topics. As is so often the case when someone is trying to rope you into a volunteer job like this, he downplayed the time commitment, exaggerated the importance of the role, and promised unending assistance in completing the task. I took the bait and agreed, not appreciating how daunting a task it is to find 46 (you get six freebies due to pre-assignments and a couple of "no-meeting Wednesdays") interesting speakers.

By using the same trickery, wile, and guile that Charlie had used on me, I was able to recruit a hardworking Program Committee and we were able to recruit the requisite number and caliber of speakers to have a successful Rotary year, at least so far as the weekly program was concerned. So successful, it seems, that my name came up several years later as a potential president, leading to breakfast at the Over Easy. Once again, the delegation from the nominating committee downplayed the time commitment, exaggerated the importance, and promised to help share the burden. Whether forgetful, gullible, or just plain stupid, I swallowed the bait (again). The members went along with the idea, and I took the gavel as president in July of 2015.

During the time leading up to and including my year as president of the Downtown Rotary, I learned a lot more about a world with which I had been affiliated for over 20 years but about which I had been largely ignorant. For most of that time, like many, maybe most, members of the club, the vast majority of my attention was focused on the weekly meetings—how good the speaker was, did the presider tell a good joke, did I make any new contacts, did they have that great chocolate-covered cheesecake on the dessert table. For me, it was all about the camaraderie, and hearing (usually) good speakers address interesting (for the most part) topics.

All along I knew that our group offered several service opportunities—bell ringing beside the kettle for the Salvation Army around Christmas and the occasional fundraisers when a natural disaster created a noteworthy need at one of our sister clubs near the site of the hurricane/earthquake/plague/pestilence. I might have been vaguely aware that we were a local outpost of a larger organization. After all, I got a glossy monthly magazine in the mail from Rotary International, but I always managed to play hooky from the meeting each September when the Rotary district governor came to speak about the condition and good works of Rotary International. Had I been paying attention, I would have realized that I was a part of something much bigger than a weekly lunch club with speeches.

I knew that the Rotary motto was "Service Above Self," but I had been largely unaware of the many ways my club put that principle into practice. Had I taken the time to get involved, I would have seen, and taken part in, a menu of community service efforts ranging from providing daily pre-kindergarten learning classes and high school career counseling to cancer screening projects in Sri Lanka and creating a walking trail in a blighted area of downtown Birmingham. In addition, I would have realized that the $50 per quarter that I had been paying as voluntary add-on to my quarterly bill was going to fund an international foundation that had, among other worthwhile initiatives, led the effort to eradicate polio from the face of the planet.

Now, as the new sucker, I mean designated leader, I am getting a crash course in the world of Rotary. As I get up to speed in my new role, going through the chairs as president-elect nominee, president-elect, and then president, my eyes are opened to a vast organization made up of over 1.2 million members in more than 35,000 local Rotary clubs, organized into approximately 530 districts in 34 zones spread across over 200 countries worldwide. While most of those clubs have fewer than 30 members, many, like ours, have more than 200 dues payers.

As part of my training process, I attend mandatory president-elect training (PET for short) sponsored by my district (6860) and three neighboring districts. In addition to learning how to lead a group (finally), I learned that all of the 100 or so clubs represented, no matter how small, are engaged in a variety of projects designed to serve the common weal. The club projects are widely varied, including digging clean water wells in Central America, gathering used eyeglasses for distribution to people who can't afford to buy them for themselves in rural Tennessee, and providing temporary housing (sort of glorified tents) to tornado victims in Alabama.

At many of the booths, the Rotary "Four-Way Test" is on display. Rotary International describes the Four-Way Test as a nonpartisan and nonsectarian ethical guide for members to use for their personal and professional relationships. At many local clubs, the members recite it at each meeting:

Of the things we think, say, or do:
- *Is it the truth?*
- *Is it fair to all concerned?*
- *Will it build goodwill and better friendships?*
- *Will it be beneficial to all concerned?*

For many Rotarians, the Four-Way Test embodies the common core that runs throughout all clubs around the world.

As my education continues, I attend an information-sharing meeting of large Rotary clubs from around the country. At this meeting in San Antonio, I am exposed to the different challenges faced by large groups (as measured by number of members) when compared to the more prevalent smaller groups. At this confab, there are lots of breakout sessions with topics ranging from increasing member engagement to the effective use of social media.

In one of the breakouts on building membership, several of the large club presidents focus on a consistent problem—many members choose to drop out of Rotary as soon as they retire from their day jobs. Many Rotary clubs, whether small, medium, or large in size, constantly face this issue and it is not without irony. Just as a member reaches a stage in life where he or she presumably has more time available to devote to service projects, they choose to become less involved. Sometimes the decision to join the club and attend the meeting has been driven by the perception of the value to one's career derived from the networking opportunities. When the career is put on ice, these members no longer feel a drive to rub elbows. More often, the decision to resign is driven by economics. The member's employer may have footed the Rotary bill and now it will come out of the individual's pocket. Whatever the cause, these early disassociations are a thorn in the side of club leadership everywhere.

My education in all things Rotary continues with attendance at district meetings in Tuscaloosa and Huntsville. The agendas at these meetings are replete with firsthand reports of work that Rotarians are doing across Alabama to help meet the needs of their communities. In some cases, the service project is limited to helping a single family with an extraordinarily compelling story. In most of the clubs that presented, the needs were broader issues facing the local community as a whole, such as helping solve student transportation needs for entire school districts. At the district conferences, attendees get not only descriptions of the projects but also helpful pointers on how to make the projects succeed. The Rotary district leadership and, in some cases, the national organization add awards and commendations to recognize particularly innovative and impactful efforts.

Organizational meetings don't stop at the district level. The Rotary org chart has each district assigned to a zone. The zones have confabs too. In between my attendance at the district meetings, I am invited to attend a meeting of Zones 30 and 31 in Baton Rouge, Louisiana, as an observer. There, I am exposed to the grueling process of becoming a district governor. The Baton Rouge meeting also gives me a feel for the next level of the organizational hierarchy. While the meeting feels immense, with over 500 ardent attendees wearing various forms of Rotary-wear and chanting Rotary slogans, I soon realize that the confab includes representatives from only eight states. There are similar meetings being conducted throughout the year, throughout the world.

Which leads to the annual international convention. During June of my year as president, the 107th annual convention is held in Seoul, South Korea. Imagine the logistics of having 44,000 Rotarians from all over the world descend on a city. To accommodate such numbers, attendees stay in hotels as far as an hour and a half drive by bus or car away from the convention center. An army of South Korean Rotarians has volunteered as greeters and meeters and logisticians. Various events are held all over the city, but most were focused on the Goyang Kintex Exhibition Center. Kintex is a complex east of downtown Seoul covering over 26 acres. The Rotary Convention seems to use every foot. In addition to speeches and presentations about good works being performed (or funded) by Rotarians around the globe, there are speeches by world-renowned authorities on a wide variety of topics. Also, the organizers go to great lengths to showcase the cultural offerings of Seoul. The planning and execution speaks volumes about the seriousness with which many Rotarians take the responsibilities of membership.

This scene is repeated about a year later when, as chairman of the Downtown Rotary, I attend the 2017 Annual Convention in Atlanta, Georgia. In Atlanta, closer to 50,000 members show up to join the festivities. Particularly well attended is the annual Rotary Peace Conference, where Rotarians from around the world explore avenues to bridge cultures and foster nonviolent solutions to issues. Much of the rest of the Atlanta convention follows the same script as the 2016 convention in Seoul, but with new speakers, some new topics, and a Southern accent.

As I talk to folks at the Atlanta convention, I am struck by the fact that the same subset of Rotarians seem to be repeat visitors to each convention. There are additions and subtractions each year, of course, but there seems to be a core group that uses the conventions as a good excuse to visit other countries and locales. The converse of this statement is that the vast majority of Rotary members never attend these meetings. Similarly, the district and zone meetings seem to be populated mostly by members who hold or hope to hold leadership positions within Rotary. For the rank and file, their service club is the weekly meetings and service projects.

While my year as president of the Downtown Rotary involves a good deal of travel and a great deal of learning, my primary responsibility is to prepare for and conduct the weekly meetings. I have witnessed many different styles over the many administrations that have spanned my tenure with the Downtown Rotary. In my view, the better presiders at the weekly meetings have been those who have injected humor into conducting the meetings, and that is my plan. My hope is that I make this part of the job look easy. It isn't.

As with so many life experiences, the more preparation that goes into a job, the smoother it runs and the more it appears to be effortless. Without question, the difficulty was lessened by having a full-time club director, Susan Jackson, who takes care of the day-to-day administrative matters. Nevertheless, each meeting requires several hours of preparation time for me, separate and apart from attendance at committee meetings, board meetings, and a variety of other recurring tasks. All of it is very rewarding, but also very time-consuming.

For me, the biggest dividend for all of the time I devote to executing my responsibilities as president is the chance to spend a little time each week with the speakers before they take the podium. (I find that a small percentage of the presenters, even some of the most accomplished, want to concentrate on their remarks rather than chitchat during the few minutes immediately preceding their talks. I try to respect their wishes in this regard.) In part because of the Rotary Club of Birmingham's reputation of consistently packing the room with up to 500 community leaders each week, we consistently draw exceptional speakers for our Wednesday lunches.

As a result, my lunch companions during the year range from the CEO of Coca-Cola to His Royal Highness, the Duke of Gloucester to the Chair of the International Habitat for Humanity to the CEO of the Talladega Superspeedway. We also heard from the Governor of Alabama, Robert Bentley, who was just beginning to realize that the impeachment hounds were nipping at his heels, and the junior U.S. Senator from Alabama, Jeff Sessions, who gave us the first public hint that he would become the first sitting Senator to endorse presidential candidate Donald Trump. (Of course, about 12 months later, Trump would swear in Sessions as the Attorney General of the United States.) After finishing up the grueling year, I was satisfied that the programs presented were topical, interesting, and diverse in both content and perspective.

My experience as the leader of the Downtown Rotary had been rewarding and fulfilling, but I can't help but wonder if my experience was an outlier. Was my year at the helm representative of what goes on only in a very large club? Moreover, was the whole organizational landscape and community service direction unique to clubs that are chartered under the Rotary banner?

To answer some of these questions, I reach out to Dan Bundy. Dan is the city president of a mid-size Alabama commercial bank. What makes Dan unique for purposes of my inquiry is that, over his career, he has been a member of four different Rotary Clubs—a small suburban club that meets in the morning, a medium-size suburban lunch club, a medium-size downtown breakfast club, and a very large urban lunch club. He has been president of three of these clubs and has been an assistant governor of Rotary District 6860. To top it all off, his father was a Rotarian. He has a unique insight into the wonders of the world of Rotary as well as the challenges faced by a service club in the 21st century.

He, like many others, originally joined a local Rotary strictly to build his circle of business contacts and to network. The service aspects of membership in Dan's early days were secondary. He remembers that when he first joined, all of the service clubs were all male. That has changed, although the international Rotary organization still hasn't had a female president.

Dan immediately identifies the biggest recurring challenge for virtually every Rotary club—the perpetual need to recruit new members and retain the old. Rotary International provides all sorts of materials designed to help clubs in their recruitment efforts. The key in his view, though, is having a vibrant club with an engaged membership and energized leaders.

From Dan's perspective, it is particularly intriguing to observe how different clubs have different personalities. He tells of his experience with two clubs in District 6860 (essentially, a geographic area comprising the northern third of the state of Alabama). One club is in the Birmingham area but fairly rural and on the smaller end with about 50 or 60 members. Despite its location and size, that club gets involved in virtually everything going on in that small community. By contrast, the second club is in a rapidly growing suburb of Birmingham. It is about the same size as the rural club but not nearly as vibrant. It is struggling to recruit new members and to find its place on the service front. Dan finds it hard to explain the differences in the DNA of the two clubs.

At the district level, Dan reports a hunger for volunteers willing to take leadership positions. The roles of district governor and assistant governor are very time-consuming, and those time commitments for a nonpaying job are off-putting to Rotarians who are also juggling a challenging career. As a result, filling these leadership ranks can be difficult and the most likely candidates are retirees.

Dan's description comes as no surprise to me. As I spend more time around the Rotary hierarchy, my observation is that progressing to the zone level is all about face time with the higher-ups in the organization. A common thread that seems to run through the stories of those who serve at the zone and international levels is that they began their treks up the Rotary leadership ladder at a fairly young age. Even for those who possess the leadership skills to be an officer at the higher levels, it takes time to progress up the chain. In some ways, it seems to be more of a longevity competition than a process designed to find the most capable leaders.

Reflecting on my conversations with Dan, I am struck by the anomaly that an organization that thrived for years as the epitome of an "old boys" club is now in many ways dependent for its survival on becoming more appealing to women and younger members. To better gain a woman's perspective on membership in a traditional service club, I recall several conversations I had had at Rotary gatherings with Gina Crumbliss. At the same time that I served as president of the Downtown Rotary, Gina was president of the Rotary Club of Chattanooga, Tennessee, Hamilton Place. Gina's presidential year was notable in many ways, but from a gender perspective it was particularly noteworthy because all three Chattanooga clubs that year were led by women, and the president-elect of Rotary International was a man who had been president of the Downtown Chattanooga club.

Gina's club would be viewed as larger than average in the world of Rotary with about 75 members. She estimates that the average age of her members was "young," in their early 50s. As with most service clubs, her club is active on the service front, both locally and internationally, with projects ranging from providing latrines in Haiti to hosting an annual Christmas party at a local children's home. Gina describes her club as being very focused on serving the community.

As for gender breakdown, the Hamilton Place club is about 30% women and 70% men. She was the third woman to have served as president of her club in its 25-year history. When asked if her gender posed any impediments to her success as president, she opines to the contrary: "They wanted me to succeed." She thinks that if there were ever any "good ole boys" in her club, "they have all been converted." She goes further and says that her conversations with her counterparts about their experience as female leaders at the other local clubs is consistent with hers. For all of them, gender was not an issue. As for the absence of any women in the role of president of Rotary International, Gina believes that it is only a matter of time. It will take time for the right woman candidate to rise to the top given the long lead time that climbing the international leadership ladder normally takes.

In terms of the challenges facing her club, Gina echoed many of the concerns that Dan had expressed. Recruiting new members is a huge challenge, but she says that getting newbies in the door is only the beginning. You must get them on-board and involved right away or they will lose interest. She also sees turbulent times ahead in terms of attracting younger new members. She believes: "Rotary is going to have to evolve to make it more attractive to millennials."

It turns out that the issues I faced as president of the Downtown Rotary and that Dan and Gina faced in their clubs are not unique to Rotary or to service clubs located in Alabama. The year after I finished as president of my Rotary Club, my brother, Rick, assumed the helm of Rampart Range Kiwanis Club of Colorado Springs. I called my brother to compare notes.

Rick's Kiwanis Club is at the other end of the size scale from the Downtown Rotary Club. It currently has 12 members and, much like the challenges described by Dan and Gina, constantly labors to find new members. Almost all of the members are, like my brother, retirees and view the Kiwanis Club as a way to stay active in the community. To that end, what the club lacks in size it makes up for in enthusiastic community service, such as the "Bring Up Grades" program, which recognizes elementary school students who increase their performance in reading and math. Rick says his club has had a terrible time attracting millennials and, for this reason, fears for the future of service clubs generally. I also reached out to my counterpart at the Birmingham Kiwanis Club, Nelson Bean, and learned that these same issues of recruitment and engagement are the ones he faced as president of the largest Kiwanis Club in the world.

After spending significant amounts of time both living the life of an active service club member and learning about the experiences of others in the world of service clubs, I am struck by the realization that I am witnessing somewhat of a cultural transformation. Despite the worthwhile role that service clubs have played over the past century in providing a place for people to gather, organize, and become active in learning about their communities and to provide much-needed services to those communities, the health of service clubs is flagging. Moreover, this condition is not limited to clubs in Alabama or just Rotary clubs. Membership in service clubs as a whole has been sliding since the 1950s.

One of the more thoughtful commentators on the field of service clubs, Quentin Wodon, has enumerated a number of reasons for the difficulties encountered by service clubs in recruiting and retaining members.[105] Those reasons include:

1. *Lack of resources.* Virtually every service club charges dues and fees, not to mention requests to support the club's projects financially. Because of these commitments, not everyone can afford to join. Affordability issues are particularly pronounced for younger potential members, and employers may be less inclined than in the past to reimburse these costs.

2. *Lack of time.* The time required to be even a casual member of a club can seem overwhelming, especially under the traditional weekly meeting format. Of course, there are the same number of hours in a day now as in 1950, but the way we choose to use those hours has morphed over time. Many folks, particularly those who have grown up in a world inhabited by blogs and electronic chat rooms, find more frenetic ways to hear about what is going on in the community around them. I have observed that even those who choose to devote time to attending meetings have a tendency, when the presentation gets slow, to pull out their smartphones and do an electronic check of what is going on at the office and in the outside world.

3. *Less prestige.* Membership may not have today the same prestige in local communities that it once had. I believe this factor varies widely from club to club and from community to community. I happen to live in a community that values the opportunities afforded by service clubs. As a result, membership carries with it a certain panache. But I freely recognize that other communities may view membership in a different way.

4. *Less professional networking opportunities.* Membership may not bring the same professional networking benefits that attracted members in the past, or at least there are now many more alternative ways to network professionally. Clearly, the internet has injected less personal options for individuals to develop their businesses, but I would maintain that it has also created a vacuum of face-to-face networking opportunities. Perhaps service clubs have an opportunity to project a fairly unique value proposition of giving professionals the chance to make personal contacts that current communication methods have limited.

5. *Lack of vitality and size.* Some clubs may not look attractive to younger generations; they may not be as vibrant as they used to be, especially when they are very small. For a recent college graduate or someone starting a new career, a room full of old codgers talking about retirement and today's aches and pains is not a very inviting environment. Could it be that more tweets and tats and trivia are needed to liven up the lunch crowd?

6. *Lack of interest in community service.* While Wodon expresses some disbelief that there is a real trend suggesting fleeting interest in serving the community through involvement in service or civic clubs, there can be no question that service clubs are encountering increased competition for the time, talent, and treasure of current and potential members. Every community has a plethora of opportunities to volunteer generally. It seems as if every nonprofit and worthy cause has created (or expanded) the office of Chief Development Officer and step number one is to create a board or junior board or committee to devise ways to market the organization and raise funds. Whether or not fewer people feel the need to serve, service clubs definitely are competing with an ever-expanding group of like-minded organizations.

In fact, as with so many traditional outlets, there are alternative models to established service clubs that are gaining traction and disrupting the typical paradigms. Some recent examples of nonprofit organizations that focus only on community service and skip the weekly-meeting-with-a-speaker format are the HandsOn Network and DoSomething.org. In each case, the prime targets are millennials who would like to focus on doing good in their local communities but who don't see the value in weekly networking opportunities.

So, do service clubs have a model that can survive the test of time? Throughout the service club world, leaders are struggling to answer this question in the affirmative. At the local level, individual clubs are trying a host of techniques to make their clubs more attractive to prospective members, ranging from remote access to meetings to expanding membership requirements to open the clubs to younger members. The parent organizations of these groups, both large and small, are also struggling to answer this question and to adapt to current tastes.

For purposes of my overall inquiry, however, I don't think it really matters. As of today, service clubs, whether we are talking Rotary, Kiwanis, or whichever one is most vibrant in your community, are alive and kicking. If you are not a member, chances are good, no matter where you live, that there are clubs that would love to have you join their ranks, and you should consider it, whether you are just getting started in your career or looking for post-retirement challenges. The conclusion that I reached from my experience and my poking and prodding of my counterparts in other organizations is that serious involvement in a service club can prove to be a rewarding endeavor on any of many levels, particularly as we face retirement and beyond.

The most basic attraction of virtually all service clubs is the opportunity to meet weekly (in most cases) with friends and hear interesting speakers. The weekly meetings are chock-full of social interaction, and most clubs offer a variety of ways to stay involved in, and to give back to, the community in which you live. As such, the weekly meetings are just a jumping-off point for much more active involvement in the good things your club is doing.

This is where the "service" in "service club" kicks in. For many of us who are facing a post-career lifestyle, a club can be the perfect post-retirement activity because we are able to match our personality to where the needs are. For example, depending on your interests and talents, you can choose between local service projects, organizational acumen, international service, philanthropy, team-building, leadership activities, or public speaking, and just go for it. And as you can understand from my description of the challenges faced by many clubs today, you will be welcomed with open arms.

But is there room for personal growth within a club? The answer is yes, on several levels. Certainly there is a path of increasing levels of involvement starting with volunteering to participate in a service project up to and including becoming a leader in the governance of the club. But pursuit of a leadership role in a service club, as with any volunteer-led organization, is a finite track. The leadership ladder at the local level is usually a three- or four-year process, with a year or two of service as somewhat of a figurehead as chairman or immediate past president. At that point, you re-enter the fold and take your seat in the audience with the rest of your friends.

One exception to this process can be found in the international clubs that encourage members to keep going up the ladder. For Rotary, this includes the district leadership, the zone leadership, and the international board; even the role of international president is a brass ring that entices many. And don't forget that most of the international service clubs have affiliated charitable foundations that support their efforts with funding. These many foundation boards also need committed members and leaders.

While the leadership track offers a high-profile, but limited, opportunity to set and achieve personal goals, service clubs offer infinite opportunities to get involved in community activities that provide worthwhile service. The model of periodic get-togethers, usually weekly meetings with a group that has a common stated purpose of providing service, is prime for getting on board with a collective attempt to achieve some meaningful purpose. Rarely do you find a club that is "between projects," but, if you do, you can always suggest your own. If anything, I have found that clubs have a tendency to overcommit and spread their limited resources too thin.

One advantage of joining one of the larger, international organizations like Rotary, the Lion's Club, or Kiwanis is the chance to provide service on a global scale. This multicultural aspect is appealing to some who want to have an impact beyond their communities, thus bringing the world together a little, perhaps with a dash of international travel thrown in. For some, the appeal to such projects is the chance for social interaction with people from different cultures, religions, and backgrounds working together to solve a problem. An obvious prime example of such a project is the multi-decade effort by Rotary International to abolish the disease of polio from the face of the earth.

Polio eradication is a great example of a high-profile effort to attack a global scourge, but there are a multitude of other lower profile international projects currently underway at each of the large service organizations. A great example of just such a project that started locally but is having salutary effects on the other side of the globe is the Rotary effort to provide cancer screening services to lower income women in Sri Lanka. It provides a good case study in how an individual with unique skill sets can leverage the international service club model to magnify the results of his or her efforts.

In this example, the Rotary member in question is Dr. Ed Partridge. Until he retired in July of 2017, Ed spent most of his time and made his living running the Comprehensive Cancer Center of Alabama. Ed's reputation in fighting cancer extends well beyond Alabama, however, and he actually spent a year as the elected volunteer president of the American Cancer Society from 2010 to 2011. Ed is also a member of the Rotary Club of Birmingham, but he came to the world of Rotary in a somewhat unusual way almost entirely because of the service opportunities that membership provides.

In 2009, Ed was approached by a group of Rotarians from the Downtown Rotary to help with a project that they had stumbled across. During a recent international fellowship visit, a Downtown Rotary delegation had visited a sister club in Colombo, Sri Lanka, and had learned of a project that had been started by that club, the largest in that island country. The members of the Rotary Club of Colombo had learned breast cancer in that country accounts for 25% of the deaths of women and that one reason was the lack of early detection of the disease.

The Colombo Club had a dream of building a public clinic where women and men (yes, men are susceptible to breast cancer too) could get mammograms, free of charge. The club had raised the necessary funds twice but had been derailed twice, once by the needs that arose from the tsunami of 2004 and once by the resettlements that resulted from the culmination of the long civil war. The need for early cancer screenings remained constant during these times of national turmoil and rose back to the top of the Colombo club's list of priorities. This time, they pitched their plan to their Rotarian counterparts from Birmingham and asked for help.

To learn how best to help with the transfer of equipment, technology, and know-how to a country on the other side of the planet, the Birmingham Rotarians turned to non-Rotarian Ed because of his international stature as a leading oncologist, and his passion for solving disparity issues in medicine, particularly in the detection and treatment of cancer. Ed immediately realized the issues faced by low-income Sri Lankan women who lacked access to early scans and tests, and the enormous impact that could be realized with a relatively small investment of funds. He agreed to help.

At first, Ed simply shared his expertise with the Birmingham Rotary team to select, purchase, ship, and install a mammography machine and other detection equipment in a special facility provided by the Colombo Rotarians. In that clinic, Sri Lankans could get precision testing, free of charge. Soon, Colombo Rotarians were visiting Birmingham to meet with Ed and the Birmingham Rotary committee.

Ed gradually became more and more involved in the joint project. When asked by the Birmingham club to travel to Sri Lanka to strengthen the relationships with the Colombo club, to meet the medical professionals working with the "Cancer Prevention and Early Detection Center," and to evaluate the project's impact, he and his wife, Barbara, never hesitated. At almost the same time, Ed accepted the invitation from the membership committee to join the Rotary Club of Birmingham and soon he was spearheading the Sri Lanka project.

Ed and his fellow Rotarians soon realized that the project needed to expand in scope to include other kinds of cancer and the sharing of cancer patient-related data. The group also envisioned expanding the project's geographical reach, making scans available to people outside the Colombo area, and its impact. With Ed's leadership on a Global Grant application submitted by four Rotary clubs on three continents (Rotary Clubs of Colombo, Nuremberg-Sigena, Zurich-Sihltal, and Birmingham, Alabama), the joint project now includes two mammography machines and two digital film processors (in Colombo and Kurunegela), an ultrasound machine, colposcopy equipment, a special chair and equipment to test for head and neck cancers, a human papillomavirus and DNA testing machine, 7,000 test kits, an electronic data-collection system with handheld devices, signage, and printed materials. To date, tens of thousands of women in Sri Lanka have been screened for breast cancer. In the first two years alone, 30,000 women were scanned on the first mammography machine in Colombo. The new equipment became operational in late 2016, and the overall results are just beginning to be tabulated.[106]

Recognizing the success of the project, Rotary's unique international service platform, and the Rotarian network to disseminate information as well as administer products, Ed has now presented another potential dimension to the cancer prevention project. One of his fields of expertise is cervical cancer and its cause—the human papillomavirus (HPV). During his work on the Cancer Prevention and Early Detection Center project, he learned much about Sri Lanka, its high literacy rate, its contained population, and the committed Rotarians there. He also saw that, while the mammography machine in Colombo was getting a lot of use, transportation systems in this small country make it difficult for poorer women in the rural areas to get mammograms or other medical services. Ed firmly believes that the Rotary network may provide one solution to this problem.

He has discussed with the Colombo and Birmingham clubs what he sees as a real possibility—Rotarians coming together to eradicate cervical cancer throughout Sri Lanka. The possibility of eradicating cervical cancer throughout the country was presented to the Rotary Club of Colombo and to its Rotary district leadership.

Since then, Colombo Rotarians on its Cancer Prevention Committee have met with their Rotary district governor and other Rotary leaders and the Sri Lankan Minister of Health, who has given his enthusiastic support. A two-pronged strategy is being formulated now—to immunize and screen for cervical cancer throughout the island country.

Ed and all of his Rotary friends have high hopes for success. This is a true win/win/win situation and a great example of how to leverage opportunities offered by a large service international club. Moreover, Ed's case provides a perfect illustration of how a service club can be used as a launching pad to leverage its members' skill sets and aspirations.

While there may be a certain level of appeal to the international aspects and altruistic stature of fighting cancer on the other side of the globe, there are plenty of local, low-budget projects that can provide just as much self-satisfaction. One of the annual efforts of the Rampart Range Kiwanis Club is a soap-box derby that gives local children and their dads a way to be creative and competitive. In Brunswick, Maine, each year the lunchtime Rotary Club provides local low-income children with pencil boxes stuffed with school supplies before school starts in the fall. Neither of these projects is as sexy as fighting cancer in Sri Lanka, but both are very important to the providers and the recipients of the services.

To be clear, as with participation in any organization, there may be certain downsides to involvement with a service club. If your only goal is to provide community service, weekly meetings with speakers and introductions and recited mantras may seem like a waste of time. You may believe that it is more efficient to skip the "middle man" and find a worthwhile cause that accepts volunteers and puts them straight to work. And the monthly club dues and assessments can add up—money that you feel could be put to better use at a particular charity.

Moreover, the nature of any organization with limited officer tenure is that you wind up with a lot of projects du jour that get started and don't ever seem to get finished. Each administration has a theme, and it changes with the next administration. Rotary has been successful to a certain extent in fighting this tendency by adopting some big overarching goals, like eradicating polio. Nevertheless, it may seem that your local club has a number of half-completed initiatives piling up. There is no question that the service club model is not perfect and is not for everyone, but it is also a tried-and-true structure that has worked well for many members in many, many communities.

So, let's get down to the lick log. How does all this fit on the SCALES scale:

Social Interaction—No question that an active service or civic club can provide all of the social interaction you could ever want. At the Downtown Rotary, in addition to the weekly meetings, there is a steady stream of service projects that entail additional opportunities to get together with other members, as well as members of the larger community. If you are willing to serve on one of the many committees that tend to functional areas, such as community or international service, you can throw in enough committee meetings and extracurricular conversations to make you wonder if you have time for your "real job." And if that isn't enough, there are monthly mixers to give you a little bar time with your Rotary buddies.

Of course, it should go without saying that attendance is important to generate the desired interaction. Moreover, you must fight the urge to sit with the same group of friends each week and volunteer for the projects that minimize social contacts. Service clubs provide ample opportunities for you to get out of your comfort zones and expand your networks. It is up to you to seize these opportunities. On this element, Rotary gets a nine.

Concentration—If you have good weekly speakers with stimulating topics, you may have to think. Other than that, mental calisthenics are not mandatory to be a good club member. Service on committees may also require you to think through the issues the committee faces. Some of those may be challenging, others more mundane, depending on the committee. The broad range of service opportunities provided by most service clubs certainly provide you a chance to pick the activity that will present a chance to use your innate talents and require you to focus.

If you rise through the ranks of club leadership, mere management of the club may provide challenges that require you to come up with innovative approaches, but you are rarely exploring new territory. You also should not underestimate the amount of effort that it takes to run a meeting every week, especially if you want it to be mildly entertaining for your members, but this challenge has a finite tenure. The rest of the time you are mostly listening, but listening to largely thought-provoking topics. As a result, in my book, participation in service clubs gets a seven in concentration.

Accomplishment—As with most pursuits, it is what you make it. If you choose to pursue a regional, national, or international leadership position, that track can provide many years of ever-increasing responsibility with an almost endless series of roles. Unfortunately, it seemed to me to be more like a longevity contest than truly engaging challenges, but one of our goals here is, after all, to live longer. Therefore, engaging in a longevity contest to score higher in the ultimate contest for longevity seems to make some sense. Based on this bit of circular reasoning, I'll give Rotary a six in accomplishment.

More to the point, the right approach to membership can lead to endless accomplishments (and potential extra points for spirituality). If you are participating in the club only for the networking opportunities, the worth of the membership dramatically dissipates when you slow down your professional life. If, on the other hand, you are driven by the chances to get organized with others and serve the community, you have hit the motherlode with the service club model. Roll up your sleeves and get to work. Whether you decide to participate on the leadership track or with community service work, service clubs are a great way to accomplish your needs in this area.

Laughter—This is another element that is in part determined by the club you choose, and how you approach your role in it. Some service clubs formally include humor on the weekly agenda. In other clubs, like the Downtown Rotary, it is largely up to the president to set the tone. Several years ago, my Rotary club had a Presbyterian preacher as president. He started every meeting with a good, clean joke. God only knows where he found 40-plus good, **clean** jokes, but almost all were genuine gut-busters.

During my year as president, I put an emphasis on humor in my weekly remarks, but I stayed clear of jokes. I think my members had a good time, and there were lots of laughs. I know that I had a good time and, while coming up with the humor required a great deal of effort each week, it made my job more enjoyable. For these reasons, Rotary gets high marks in the laughter category. I give it a seven.

Exercise—I suppose some of the service projects involve efforts that could pass as exercise, but most of the reps in these workouts involve lifting the fork and bending the elbow. Here we have another case of a pastime being whatever you decide to make it. The plethora of service opportunities include many that require physical exertion. But there is rarely a movement to add a high-intensity interval training question to the Four-Way Test. A score of two is exceedingly generous.

Spirituality—Each Rotary meeting begins with a nondenominational invocation at the start of the weekly meetings of the Rotary Club of Birmingham, and there is the occasional speaker with a spiritual-ish message, but it would be hard to say that the Downtown Rotary promotes spiritual encounters. Other service clubs, especially those with an affiliation to particular religious denominations such as the Knights of Columbus, likely have a deeper spiritual dimension. Others, maybe less. But once again, this element depends in large part on what you make of it.

For example, the Downtown Rotary supports several service projects that help others and give members who participate a sense of gratitude. In those cases, the spiritual aspects of club membership come to the forefront and you get a real sense of why they are called "service" clubs. Unfortunately, the higher you rise in the ranks, the farther away you are from the rank and file, and you find yourself reading the reports about the meaningful work that is being done rather than seeing it firsthand. Based on my experience, I would give Rotary a six on the element of spirituality.

Plugging all of these ratings into my handy-dandy matrix, my membership in a service club produces a composite score of 7.2. Without doubt, depending on individual predilections, working with such a club provides a means of achieving all of the elements necessary to increase the odds of a long and healthy life. Unless you volunteer for the committee that walks the highways and byways and picks up litter, if you choose to devote your life to service club work, you may need to augment your activities with a physical fitness regimen. Otherwise, you likely can find the rest of the ingredients needed for a successful retirement.

Personally, I need to keep looking within my service club world for the type of involvement that will allow me to achieve the flow that I am looking for. The preparation and public speaking aspects of my year as president provided that experience, but that was a finite experience that is not easily replicated. I haven't given up yet. There are lots of opportunities here to find the right niche.

But you should always keep in mind the many advantages of seeing your friends on a regular basis.

Two older ladies had been friends and members of the same Lions Club for many decades. Over the years, they had shared all kinds of activities and adventures. Lately, their activities had been limited to their weekly club meetings.

One day, they were having their weekly lunch together when one looked at the other and said, "Now don't get mad at me. I know we've been friends for a long time, but I just can't think of your name! I've thought and thought, but I can't remember it. Please tell me what your name is."

Her friend glared at her. For at least a minute she just stared and glared.

Finally, she said, "How soon do you need to know?"

12

Heading for Hoover

Warren Lightfoot is a retired lawyer. For over 40 years, he worked hard at his profession and built a reputation as a top-notch litigator. In 1996, the esteem with which other lawyers held him manifested itself in his election to the position of president of the Alabama Bar Association. At the national level, he served as president of the American College of Trial Lawyers, one of the most prestigious subsets a litigator can achieve. Let's just agree that Warren knocked it out of the park as a lawyer. On January 1, 2008, at the age of 69, he walked out of the door of the law firm that he had established in 1990, Lightfoot Franklin & White, and retired.

The abruptness of Warren's decision to retire was somewhat unusual. Typically, a lawyer in private practice will slow down over a number of years and then phase out of the everyday practice of law. Many times the shift will take years, maybe decades. In fact, one of the "advantages" touted for a career in law, as opposed to, say, medicine, is that you don't ever have to retire—you can practice law until the day you die. Yippee!

Warren foundered for some time after he quit the law. He had thought that he would turn sculpting, a pastime that he had pursued for many years, into a sort of full-time pursuit. While it was a pleasant pastime, he found that it was not an adequate replacement for the intellectual challenges and social engagement he had enjoyed as an attorney. Almost by chance, he fell into the world of duplicate bridge as a passion to pursue in retirement.

He had played a little bit of bridge years before as a way to pass the time when he was being processed out of the Army, but had given the game up for the challenges of finding and building a career and raising a family. Some six months after his turn-my-back-on-work date, he was on a visit to a popular mountain getaway when he stumbled upon a group of friends playing "party bridge." They were playing each hand for small sums of money and were eager to welcome a new chump into their circle.

Before long, Warren discovered that the more serious players in his group also undertook a more serious form of the game on a more seriously regular basis: duplicate bridge. Party bridge, as the name implies, has a very social aspect, where partners are usually assigned based on the luck of the draw and that same luck may or may not extend to the cards drawn with each hand. Duplicate bridge is a version of the game in which you and your partner will play the exact same hands as all the other twosomes. Throughout a session, you team up with the same partner. Ideally, you and your partner play together with enough regularity to develop an understanding about how to bid and play the various combinations of cards that you're dealt. Some duplicate bridge partnerships, where there is an exceptionally good personality fit, may last for decades.

In duplicate bridge, you can't blame a bad score on the luck of the draw, because every team plays the same cards in each match. Your performance is gauged by how well you do relative to all the other players in the room. If you get a crappy hand, you enjoy the solace that the person sitting at your chair at every other table in the room at some point during the sessions will have an equally crappy hand. Also, you can't blame your performance on being assigned a lousy partner. The two of you chose each other and have chosen to stay together, at least for one more bridge match.

This intellectual challenge appealed to Warren, and he got hooked. He also found some appeal in the fact that each time he played, he could win points toward the designation of "Master." These points would accumulate whenever he did well at playing, so long as he was playing in an event sanctioned by the American Contract Bridge League. While it typically takes many years for the average player to achieve this level, the goal was something that fired Warren's jets.

He joined the Birmingham duplicate bridge league and found a partner out of the group of party bridge players. He and his partner took to participating in the official games at the clubhouse on a two to three games a week schedule. Such outings typically last three to four hours, but Warren says the time flies. In addition, he says that when he leaves he feels the same sort of mental stimulation and exhilaration that he felt leaving law school exams 50 years ago.

The discussion with Warren about duplicate bridge was actually the continuation and expansion of a conversation I had had with my sister-in-law Ann Nelson, several years before. During a visit to her home in Colorado Springs, I learned about her obsession with duplicate bridge. She showed me the latest copy of the monthly magazine that comes to her as a member of the American Contract Bridge League. She pointed out that the mailing label on the cover includes the number of points she has accumulated toward her quest to become a Master Bridge Player. She went on to describe a vibrant subculture in C-Springs devoted to the obsession of playing duplicate bridge. At the time, I was intrigued and found her compulsion amusing, but returned home from my visit and re-immersed myself in my career. Now, approaching a different stage of life, I find duplicate bridge has resurfaced, this time as a viable pursuit.

I call Ann Nelson the weekend after Warren gave me his pitch for bridge and ask her how to learn the game from a duplicate perspective. She directs me to the American Contract Bridge League website, and I start working my way through ACBL *Learn to Play Bridge – Course 1*.[107] With my typical under-appreciation for the difficulty of tasks that others can make look easy, I think I can knock Course 1 out in a weekend. Instead, I wind up investing closer to 80 hours in the process. Moreover, while I learn a good deal about the basics of bridge, I learn nothing about the niceties of duplicate bridge. One of the last instructions in the e-book is, in essence, "Now, go get some in-person lessons."

That task is not as easy as it sounds. I quickly learn that unlike playing the piano, bridge is not easily taught in one-on-one lessons. To really get the hang of it and receive the maximum benefit, you need a whole group of wannabes. To get that group setting, I learn that I need to sign up at the duplicate bridge gathering place. Thus begins my trip down the rabbit hole of duplicate bridge. First stop—the

Birmingham Duplicate Bridge Club, in Hoover, Alabama, a suburb about 15 miles south of downtown Birmingham. There, you can join a beginning bridge course taught by the unsinkable Jeanne Wamack.

The best way to describe Jeanne (or Queen Jean as she sometimes describes herself in her lesson book *Building Bridges*[108]) is to continue the analogy of *The Sound of Music*. Try to imagine Fraulein Maria reincarnated as an ebony-haired, ebullient bridge nanny with a lilting Southern accent. Instead of teaching music with catchy phrases like "Doe, a deer, a female deer...," Queen Jean teaches the finer points of bridge with mnemonic devices like "Boston—bottom of something, top of nothing" or "PIG—Pass, Invite, Game" or "Odd gets the nod, even—I'm leavin." Jeanne is always upbeat, and she finds duplicate bridge to be a never-ending, stimulating, intellectual challenge. In addition to teaching the game, she regularly participates in bridge tournaments around the Southeast.

Jeanne's course consists of a lesson a week for 13 weeks. She offers it twice a year. It just so happens that she is starting a set of classes the following week, and I decide to give it a try. There are two options available: 9:30 on Monday mornings or, with a one-week lag in course materials, 6:30 on Tuesday evenings. Given my full-time work schedule, I assume that the night class will be the better course, but it comes as a (stupid) shock to learn just how many Tuesdays I am either out of town or committed to social and business entertainment. This overcommitted schedule issue is compounded by rush hour traffic on the road to Hoover that makes Tuesday evenings a difficult proposition. As a result, I find myself slipping out of the office on Mondays to slide down to the BDBC clubhouse for a two-hour bridge lesson with 15 to 20 mostly "advanced middle-aged," mostly retired but enthusiastic students who, like me, want to explore the mysteries of duplicate bridge.

The BDBC is housed in a comfortable nondescript building in a warehouse district of Hoover about a mile off Interstate 65. The building has several rooms containing dozens of card tables. The rooms can be configured for various size groups and several concurrent games for players with varying skill levels. Jeanne's lessons are taught in a comfortable room that easily can accommodate a class of 32 students divided into eight tables of four. She makes use of a large rolling grease board to sketch out different possible hands to explain bidding and play of the cards. The first hour or so of each class is devoted to instruction, with the second hour or so engaged in actual play of hands that have been carefully prearranged to illustrate the lessons of the day.

Queen Jean stresses repeatedly that what she is really trying to do is teach you how to talk to your partner through everything you do so that the two of you, to the maximum extent possible (without cheating), learn what each of you has in the hands you have been dealt. Any bid you make (or, if you pass, don't make), or card you play, is imbued with meaning. A particular opening bid may indicate strength in a particular suit, or a large number of cards in a suit without any high face cards. In some cases, a bid is considered "forcing" in that the bidder's partner must come back with some response and may not simply pass, no matter how weak the responder's hand. Other bids are merely invitational or probative. Other bids are considered "cuebids," meaning that you raise the bid in your opponents' suit to signal to your partner that you have support for your partner's suit and some strength in your hand. Sometimes you are even allowed expressly to make sure of the meaning. For instance, when your partner bids one no-trump, you are allowed to declare, "15 to 17 high card points."

Over the years certain accepted series of bids have developed. Known as "conventions," the sequence that follows a particular trigger bid is designed to elicit specific information about your partner's holdings and may be entirely unrelated to the cards specified. By way of example, if it is obvious from the bidding that both you and your partner have good hands, and the opposition does not, you can take the bidding to the next level of information gathering by bidding four "no-trump." Your partner (hopefully) knows that you have just signaled that you want to use the Blackwood Convention to explore the contents of your partner's hand. In other words, this bid is code for "we both have huge freaking hands, and we need to figure out if it's possible that we could take every freaking trick." (Note that bridge players do not use profanity.)

If your partner comes back with a bid of five clubs, it does not mean anything about the clubs in her hand. Instead, your partner has just told you that she has either zero or four aces. If, instead, she bids five diamonds, five hearts, or five spades, the responses mean one, two, or three aces respectively. If you determine that your side has all the aces, you can take it a step further and ask about kings by coming back with a five no-trump bid, and her response will follow the same pattern only this time describing the number of kings in her hand.

Sound complicated? It is. But this is a pretty extreme example because hands with cards distributed in a way that warrant application of the Blackwood Convention are pretty rare. My point here is that the duplicate bridge rabbit hole is exceedingly deep. You can have fun and find a challenge with just a basic knowledge of the rules, but there seem to be endless ways to hone your skills. As you get better and your ease of communication with your partner increases, you discover more and more conventions to take those conversations-in-play to new heights of dialogue.

While the rules of bridge permit and, in many cases, encourage certain verbal and nonverbal communication, other forms of passing secret messages are expressly forbidden, such as tugging at your ear or playing a card with a suggestive angle. The lore passed around the bridge table often includes tales of players who have devised crafty ways to telegraph information about their hands only to be found out by the officials at the tournament and unceremoniously drummed out of the competition. One of the goals of Jeanne's lessons is to teach you what you can and can't do under the rules, thereby sparing you the embarrassment of being chastised publicly at the games and tournaments by the official referee, known as the Director.

If all of this seems exceedingly confusing then I have succeeded in conveying a small part of the dismay that I and the others in Queen Jean's class feel each week. In essence, we are learning a new language—a language that is a cross between solving calculus, practicing sign language, divining tea leaves, and mind-reading. In this new language, bids and the order of play form paragraphs, but always subject to interruption and reconfiguring by the opponents. Jeanne also makes clear from the outset that other teachers and Master players ascribe different meanings to certain hands, bids, and card plays. In fact, I had noticed on the first day that there are slight but significant differences between Jeanne's bidding rules and those I had learned in the ACBL *Learn to Play Bridge—Course 1*.

Over the course of the ensuing weeks I learn several additional lessons (many not having anything to do with the game):

1. It is hard to pursue bridge AND a full-time job at the same time. If this is the road to happiness, I need to do something about my paying job.

2. Duplicate bridge players come from all walks of life. Ike Eisenhower was one. Warren Buffet is one. In Queen Jean's classes I have met a medical doctor who used to teach at Tufts, a former ear/nose/throat doctor, a retired bank teller, a security guard from a local hospital, a homemaker, and a lamp salesman.
3. Most learners come to the day class. I suppress the horrifying thought that this is because the 6:30 p.m. to 8:30 p.m. class may cause us to stay up past our bedtimes.
4. Slow bridge players are excruciating. I am reminded of the adage a friend once taught me about golf: A bad golfer is always welcome in a foursome with good golfers—provided, however, that the bad golfer must play fast and never try to look for his lost golf balls. Surely, there is a corresponding adage in bridge.

As the weeks pass, I am becoming increasingly anxious to test-drive my new bridge skills in an actual game. My chance comes when Jeanne announces that the next week she will be playing in a tournament and all of her students are invited to join "Mike's Game," which takes place each week at the same time as Jeanne's class in an adjacent room.

Mike, it seems, is charged with conducting the next step in the learning process. His game consists of a short (10- to 15-minute) lecture, followed by 10 to 12 hands of bridge. Many of Mike's players are graduates of Jeanne's programs. Others have played party bridge for years and want to pursue another variant of the game.

"Party bridge" is a somewhat derisive term that duplicate bridge players use to describe the game as played by those smaller groups just for fun and an excuse to socialize. In such games, the deal of the cards at each table is totally random. The stakes may be high if the participants wish to put cash on the table, but the payouts are based on each partnership's success against the other team at that table (as opposed to the entire room). In some party bridge settings the players may be intent and serious, but the randomness of the deal injects a degree of luck into the game.

This format seems to elicit condescension from duplicate devotees, who view it as requiring less mental discipline. In addition, many party bridgies like to, well, party while they play. Sometimes the party becomes just as important as the bridge. A couple of glasses of wine may lighten the mood at the table, but it also has a tendency to lessen the concentration. As a result, serious duplicate bridge players often look down their noses at the party bridge version of the game.

At Mike's Game, I find several of the attendees want to take their party bridge habits to the next level of addiction. Other attendees seem to be using Mike's Game as a convenient avenue for re-entering the pastime after a few years off. As with Jeanne's class, virtually everyone is of retirement age. A noticeable difference from Jeanne's group is that, of the 20 people in the room, there are only two men.

The atmosphere in Mike's room is definitely more intense than that in Jeanne's class. Where Jeanne has more of a nurturing, patient, maternal approach to duplicate bridge, Mike is more of a drill sergeant. After he maps out a bidding sequence on the large white board at the front of the class, he becomes visibly irritated if you later ask him to repeat the logic behind it. On several occasions, he prods his participants to play more quickly if the pace of play is being threatened by one slowpoke. When I incorrectly bid a hand and then have the bad luck of having: a) Mike playing on the other team at my table; b) all of my cards exposed as the "dummy"; and c) my improper bid deprive Mike of the ability to make the bid he wants, he quickly, snarkily, and audibly corrects my bid.

Beyond Mike himself, there are other, more subtle, differences in Mike's room. While everyone (other than Mike) in the room is, to one degree or another, unsure about their abilities, you notice stark variations in confidence levels. Those who have plied their skills in this arena for a while may not have gained enough experience to move to the next level, but they are the royalty in this sandbox. Sometimes this shows in the speed of play. Other times, it is the brutality with which they apply new rules of the road, as in the time my innocent newbie partner immediately wanted to retract a card she had placed on the table only to be informed that "a card laid is a card played." It is fairly easy to catch glimpses of what serious bridge play looks like. (Only afterwards do I learn that once you have accumulated 20 masterpoints, you are required to graduate from Mike's Game and fully enter the great wide-open of duplicate bridge. This fact suggests that the "royalty" have a pretty paltry realm.)

After two and a half hours, I emerge from my first visit to Mike's class, weary but unscathed. While it would be easy to find much of it unpleasant, the overall experience is very beneficial. The stakes may be low (only a few masterpoints awarded for each session), but the pressure that comes from having actual opponents playing actual hands that are not preset to practice the day's lesson forces me to reach back to rules that were described in the ACBL course and reinforced by Jeanne but never applied in real time. While the number of such rules seems overwhelming in the abstract, actual play makes them seem real and retention much easier. As with all mind matters, repetition in application is helpful.

Moving from table to table after each hand gave me new insight about how different pairs of players react to different situations, and how the "play of hand" or order that the cards are played can be just as important as the cards themselves. Also, for the first time, it becomes obvious to me how the scoring of various hands can be critical to your overall success. Even though having an instructor bark at you may not be pleasant, it does cause you to raise your game to a new level. After the fact, I learned that my randomly assigned partner and I had placed fourth out of the 10 teams that played that day.

My experience in Mike's room was somewhat of a watershed and causes me to reach several conclusions. First, it is time to move on out of the comfortable nest of "learner" and continue to spread my wings as "beginner." While I may continue to take Jeanne's classes and finish out the remaining few weeks of the course, I am prepared to go to the next level and my game will benefit. Since Mike's Game occurs each week at the same time as Jeanne's Monday class, this decision may require some difficult choices, but there seems little benefit to prolonging the inevitable leap (okay, okay—it is really just a baby step) to the next level.

Second, this game is really challenging. Learning the basic rules is a snap. Applying those rules to maximum advantage requires a good deal of strategy. I am becoming painfully aware of endless competitive opportunities that Warren Lightfoot spoke of in such excited tones several months before when he tried to explain his attraction to the games. Hopefully, some of the strategies and conventions will come more easily the more I play.

Mike's Game also opens my eyes to the issue of masterpoints. By putting an upper limit on the points accumulated by each player, Mike has ensured that only novices are competing against novices in the room, but it also introduces us to the notion that some iCloud somewhere is keeping track of us and how well we play. Kinda spooky. And what the hell is a "masterpoint" anyway?

150   Now What?

As it turns out, the concept of masterpoints introduces a whole new level of complexity of, and appreciation for, competition within the world of duplicate bridge. There are no fewer than 17 skill levels recognized by the American Contract Bridge League, ranging from Rookie (that's me) to Grand Life Master. Achievement of each rank requires accumulation of points that are awarded for performance in any match that is sanctioned by ACBL. (Currently, the ACBL recognizes about 1,200 tournaments a year nationwide.) Each level has a minimum number and "pigmentation" of required points. For instance, to become a Life Master today, a player must garner at least 500 points. Those points must comprise at least 50 gold or platinum; at least 100 red, gold, or platinum; at least 75 silver; and at least 75 black.[109]

The color assigned to points is determined by the type of match in which the points are earned. Mike's Game qualifies for only black points. Play at Sectional Tournaments at Clubs (STaC) earns silver points. Regional Tournaments run by ACBL districts give out gold and red points—the color depending on the intensity of play. At North American Bridge Championships (NABC), players can earn gold, red, or platinum points.

The number of points you can garner at any match is a function of four factors: 1) the level of the tournament (i.e., internet, local, STaC, Regional, or NABC); 2) the experience level of the group against whom you are competing as determined by the maximum number of aggregate masterpoints held by the players before the match; 3) the number of teams playing; and 4) your team's performance relative to all the other teams playing. The system carefully attempts to pit competitors of similar levels of skill against each other and make the rewards commensurate with the levels of play.

By way of example, to be eligible to participate, every player in Mike's Game must have accumulated no more than 20 points. If 12 pairs of competitors show up to play on a given day, 3.3 masterpoints will be distributed to the top five teams, with the two players in the best team each receiving .6 points and the players on the fifth place team each earning .12 points. This scheme for racking up points, at first look, can seem confusing, but to put it into perspective after my participation in seven of Mike's Games I have pocketed a grand total of 1.03 masterpoints. Life Master, here I come (if I get serious about the game and live to be 99)!

The final revelation from my early days playing in Mike's room is the increasing necessity that I find a compatible partner to play with on a regular basis. I learn the hard way that if I want to be a competitive duplicate bridge player, it does me little good to learn this new language unless I have a partner who speaks the same dialect—who has learned the same meanings, inflections, and signals. Once having reached that conclusion, I determine it imperative that I conduct a search to find a good bridge partner.

First stop is my wife to see if she would like to "cross the bridge" together. She is quick to decline the invitation (and make fun of the pun). While she sort of understands my attraction to the game, she does not share the desire to play. So much for finding marital bliss in a deck of cards.

Next, I return to Warren to see if he knows of anyone looking for a partner. He says he will ask around, but that I should be very careful as it is exceedingly difficult to fire a partner once you have picked one. He says there are no diplomatic skills sufficiently refined to conduct such a divorce without bruising feelings. I also let it be known around the law firm that I am considering taking up the game and need a partner.

Next thing I know, I get a call from Bill Hinds, a senior partner in my firm who is looking to find a partner to play some not-so-serious bridge. Unfortunately, Bill is more sizzle than steak when it comes to actually playing. We talk and talk about playing together, but never seem to get to the table. I finally awake to the reality that even if I get Bill to the club house in Hoover, each subsequent outing will be like pulling the mule to the harness. After scratching my head for several weeks at this non-starter, I abandon Bill and try another approach.

In one of my classes with Queen Jean, she makes reference to one of her recent graduates who has taken to the game with a vengeance—Margaret King. It just so happens that, while she is a good five years younger, I know Margaret and her husband socially. Rather than put Margaret on the spot (and give her husband the wrong idea about my intentions), I call her husband and inquire as to whether he plans to be her duplicate bridge partner. He says that he enjoys playing party bridge with her but is not ready to take the duplicate plunge and will send me her email address. I then reach out to Margaret directly and receive a response a few days later.

I discern a certain degree of trepidation in Margaret's answer. As seems to be the duplicate bridge tradition, she is very encouraging of my desire to take up the game, and very accommodating in helping me work through my lack of a partner, but she seems to be reluctant to put herself in any position that could lock her into a bad bridge partnership. Eventually, we agree to play together the next Monday at Mike's class.

The resulting three and a half-hour game confirms several conclusions. As before, I find the actual play vastly more enjoyable and informative than studying the books or taking the classes. Second, having an enthusiastic partner who enjoys the game and its many challenges is infectious and adds significantly to my level of enjoyment. Third, it doesn't hurt to have a teacher as a partner. I had forgotten that Margaret's career is teaching French at a local college, and she brings that same skill set (and patience) to the bridge table. The "lessons learned" discussions after playing a hand are almost as interesting as the play. All in all, playing with Margaret is a delight.

Fortunately, Margaret seems to enjoy playing with me as well. She asks me to return and play as her partner when I can. More importantly, perhaps, for the longer range likelihood that we will continue a duplicate bridge partnership in the future, she learns after the fact that we placed third out of 13 teams at our inaugural match. It looks like I passed my first test. In the ensuing weeks, we play together a few more times. Unfortunately, our budding bridge relationship doesn't last. When the summer ends, school starts and Margaret goes back to her job as a college professor.

Before returning to academia, Margaret invites me to join a couples bridge group that she has organized. She says that there almost always is a need for an extra player as one or another spouse seems to be traveling on bridge night. The locations for these Thursday night games rotate between the homes of the various couples. She kindly adds my name to the email string for weekly notices.

Two weeks later, I attend my first game with Margaret's social bridge group. It turns out that the participants don't consider this to be party bridge because the group is trying to learn the duplicate bridge rules and play more serious bridge. To further this ambition, a seasoned duplicate player is in attendance each week and she is patient with each person who comes over, interrupts her play, and asks her a question about bidding or playing their hand. We also have duplicate bridge teachers (including Queen Jean on occasion) make guest appearances to provide lessons on the finer points of the game.

Despite these attempts to inject an air of seriousness, the atmosphere is much more convivial than in Hoover (maybe the wine has something to do with that) and there seems to be more laughter than learning. For me, perhaps the biggest revelation of the night is that I seem to be much farther along the learning curve than most of the others, giving me some measure of assurance that the time I have devoted to this point is paying dividends.

While all of this is very enjoyable, I don't get the feeling that my bridge improves much from the time devoted. For one thing, there is no element of duplicate bridge in this game, so each table is playing different hands that are strictly dependent on the luck of the draw. There is also no opportunity to develop a working relationship with one bridge partner since you play with a different partner each week. There are, of course, benefits from the social interactions that come from party bridge, and I find myself making some new friends and deepening some old relationships.

Party bridge works well with me on a certain level—my schedule. Because many of the others in my bridge group are still working full-time, the games take place after normal working hours. Mike's Game, on the other hand, takes most of Monday morning. My travel schedule for work heats up in the fall, and my attendance at both games becomes intermittent, but mostly I can make only the party bridge games. A common adage in the legal profession is "The law is a jealous mistress," meaning, of course, that it is very time-consuming to be a practitioner. I am now learning that I now have two mistresses competing for my time, only one of whom pays me.

Once my work travel schedule calms down a little, I am able to return to Mike's Game in Hoover, and through serendipitous circumstances I'm paired with a semi-retired hospital administrator named Marie Garner, and we seem to play well together. She is pretty conservative in her play. Me—not so much. She has been playing party bridge for several years but has begun playing duplicate only a few months before. She seems to have the desire to get serious about the game. Perhaps most important, we get along well at the table and are both reasonably competitive while both recognizing that it is only a game. We begin to seek each other out to play each week in Mike's Game.

At the same time that I am getting comfortable with Marie as a partner at Mike's Game, I am able to attend several sessions of party bridge with Margaret's couples group. These are fun gatherings, but the actual playing of the game is clearly becoming secondary to the social aspects. Each time, I seem to be the participant who makes a point of suggesting that it is time to end the cocktail portion of the evening and commence the bridge portion.

We are all beginners, so there is a good deal of cross talk and sharing of information with partners. After most deals, there is an extensive post-mortem to determine what we all should have done if we were practiced practitioners. The play is clearly secondary to the social aspects of the gathering. I am getting the sense that, from the standpoint of evaluating bridge on the SCALES scale, party bridge may be a better way to seek out social interaction, but at the expense of the concentration that competitive bridge encourages.

Unfortunately, one result of my tricky schedule is that I am an unreliable partner and Marie finds other partners to play with on a regular basis, causing me to get a couple of reminders in the "importance-of-a-partner" department. One week, I am able to get to Mike's Game in Hoover at the last minute, but Marie is not in attendance. Only nine people show up, including me. As a result, my assigned partner is Mike himself. Mike goes out of his way to make sure that I am the one who plays each hand where we have won the bidding and the cards seem to fall our way. We win that day's match.

Several weeks later, I get to see the flip side of partnering. Marie is not available again, and I get assigned a very pleasant but overtly timid partner. We win several hands but seem to have underbid those and find that we lose a couple of hands that should have been winnable. We don't seem to gee and haw on the playing of the hands either. The result of the morning's efforts—dead last out of a group of nine teams. The next week, Marie is back and we place first out of the seven groups playing. The combination of these experiences over the space of about a month drives home the importance of having a good partner and how critical the bidding and play is to the ultimate outcome of each hand. Marie and I seem to be understanding each other's accent as we speak this new language.

I seem to have come to a flexion point in my long trial with duplicate bridge. If I hope to get to the next level of play, I need a partner whose personality and style of play works well with mine. Marie seems to fill the bill. We seem to play well together, but I sense that she is trying to assess my suitability too. She also is semi-retired and appears to have the time and the inclination to play more than the once a week that I am able to carve out of my schedule. The net result of these factors is that I seem to have reached a point in this endeavor that I need to make a decision—if I want to get serious about creating a bridge partnership and take my play to the next level, I will also need to get serious about the amount of time I devote to my "paying career."

After investing close to 150 hours learning the game, and spending over 10 months of intermittent play, I feel that I have ample knowledge to rate duplicate bridge on the SCALES scale:

Social Interaction—No question that bridge forces you to interact with a diverse group of others. While there is a tendency in party bridge to seek out people you already know, my experience with the organized duplicate variety of the game is that you are routinely thrown into a group of complete strangers, but without the social awkwardness that usually comes with first meetings. At first glance, the interactions within the game rooms are fairly superficial, but I notice that the regulars in the clubhouse seem to have deeper relationships. Even with my limited exposure to the Hoover club, as time goes by, I have gotten to know several of the other players and their stories. That certainly seems to be the case between regular partners.

The multitude of opportunities to play (at the BDBC there are over a dozen organized games each week, all sanctioned by the ACBL) provide ample opportunity for regular social interaction. In addition, similar to service clubs, there are leadership opportunities within the club itself. The BDBC has a governing board and a slate of officers to run the operations. Also, each official club game has a director, who serves as a kind of referee to make sure that the plethora of rules are applied to a match in an even-handed manner.

Clearly, duplicate bridge is a social activity with an abundance of opportunity to create and strengthen relationships with others. In my book (please pardon that pun), it deserves a score of eight.

Concentration—From the beginning of my deep dive into the world of bridge, I have been surprised by the level of thought I have had to devote. When I started my exploration of the world of duplicate bridge, I remembered my brief forays into party bridge soon after law school and considered that I already knew the basics. I assumed that I could quickly morph into a reasonably good competitor at duplicate with minimal effort. I soon learned that this game that seemed like only a pleasant excuse for older folks to gather and gossip is actually a very challenging puzzle to solve that attracts people of all ages and walks of life.

First, there is a set of rules to memorize based on the priority of the suits and the assignment of points to the high cards in your hand. Major suits (spades and hearts) win games with fewer tricks than minor suits (diamonds and clubs). A no-trump bid requires even fewer tricks to win a game. There are also a host of rules to memorize about the scores that are awarded for games versus partial-game victories, and how those scores vary depending on "vulnerability."

Once the basics are committed to memory, a player has to learn the language of bidding. My analogy of picking up bridge to picking up a new language is apt, but it fails to describe several nuances of this pursuit. As with most languages, there are degrees of understanding and difficulty. French 101 may be sufficient to order a meal in Paris and find the bathroom, but true fluency takes years of study, constant practice, and exposure to others who speak *la langue*. In addition, the language gradually changes over time. Likewise, you can learn the basics of bidding and playing bridge in fairly short order, but mastery can take years. I also learned in my first few lessons with Queen Jean that some guidelines and conventions set out in the online course offered by the ACBL had changed in the 15 years following its publication.

Of course, speaking the language is only the equivalent of arming for battle. The actual fighting also requires intense concentration. A deck of 52 cards, made up of four different suits, dealt out randomly into four hands of 13 cards, can wind up in any of 635,013,559,600 different configurations, give or take a few million.[110] Let's call that a "whole bunch." The ramification of those many possibilities is that, while you can learn how to deal with some of the more likely allocations of the cards in ways that increase your odds of outscoring your opponents, you will constantly face variations giving many options for the optimal outcome.

Stated another way, bidding may be a new language, but playing is more akin to a statistics class. The possible distributions of the cards govern the odds of success of different bidding and plays of the hands. Maximize your odds and, over time, you maximize your score. Thus, concentration is required constantly during play. This intense effort explains why, following a good game of bridge, I feel mentally drained—just as Warren Lightfoot had predicted when he convinced me to give it a try years before.

Add it all up and duplicate bridge scores a nine on concentration.

Accomplishment—Of course, much depends on the variety of bridge you choose to play (e.g., duplicate vs. party bridge), the intensity that you and your partner bring to the game, and the skill level of the opponents you take on. The good news about organized duplicate bridge is that it is a sport that recognizes that it is no fun to get your ass kicked every time you play. Accordingly, you can pick the game that corresponds to your skill level as determined by the number of masterpoints you have accumulated. The flip side of the scoring regimen is that the less accomplished the group with whom you are competing (as measured by accumulated masterpoints, of course), the fewer the number of masterpoints available to you if you win. Nevertheless, each match permits a feeling that you have made some headway toward some status as a bridgie. Moreover, the methods devised by the ACBL of pitting players against other players as a means of accumulating masterpoints is an ingenious way to add a measure of accomplishment that is quantifiable and trackable in each match.

In fairly short order, I found myself going on the club website after every game to see how I did and whether I had earned any masterpoints. Whether or not such scores amount to anything on the cosmic chart of accomplishment, my psyche seems to find them meaningful. It is this challenge that keeps Warren Lightfoot headed back to Hoover several times a week to compete and led him to encourage me to take up the game. I have found this aspect of the game an effective way to punch my challenge buttons. As a result, duplicate bridge gets a seven on this element.

Laughter—Not so much. Like many pursuits, to a certain extent the bridge environment is what you make it and you can find humor if you try. As I got to know my fellow duplicate devotees, I learned who could tell a joke and who could take a joke. Occasionally, the play (or misplay) of a particular hand might lead to a laugh. I also found that party bridge, as the name and alcohol consumption would imply, seem to involve more frivolity.

Despite the focus the game requires, most of the players I have met seem to have pretty good senses of humor and don't take themselves too seriously. My impression is that such lightheartedness dissipates as a player ascends in the rankings. Once you start playing with the serious players, the game takes on a more serious atmosphere. For the Life Masters, bridge doesn't appear to be a laughing matter in any way.

While out and out laughter is fairly rare while play is underway, it is important to stress that the endeavor, at least for me, is very enjoyable. When I have won the bidding on a hand and have to play it, I feel an odd rush of adrenaline as my partner lays down the dummy hand and my strategy unfolds in my mind. In those cases where my partner and I are trying to defeat the other team's contract, the competitive juices surge. The overall process of trying to outwit a roomful of others with roughly the same level of skill as you is very entertaining. The point here is that the laughter score for duplicate bridge needs to take into account the appeal that the game holds for me based on pure enjoyment from the pursuit. Add in a modicum of pure humor at each outing and a score of six on the laughter scale seems appropriate.

Exercise—Virtually none. The distance between the tables in most matches requires a leisurely 20-second stroll. A three-hour game may require switching tables about four or five times. Throw in a couple of trips to the bathroom and you still haven't mangaged to reach five minutes of aerobic activity. I'll be generous and give it a two only because I am getting up and out of my pajamas and going to the clubhouse to play. It seems like I ought to get some exercise credit for that activity.

Spirituality—Virtually none, unless you assign points for the prayers offered up in the hopes of improving the quality of your next bridge hand. I once played in a monthly poker game that we called a "prayer group" because one of the members was an Episcopal priest and he would offer up a prayer at the beginning of the night. Thus far, I haven't found a bridge game that offers even that level of spirituality. Accordingly, a score of one seems appropriate for this factor.

Add it all up and duplicate bridge scores 7.1 on the SCALES scale.

It is worth noting that, at least for me, bridge also seems to be an effective way for me to enter a state of flow. When I am playing, I feel fully engaged and challenged. The time required for the match passes quickly and pleasantly. If anything, I am so engrossed in play that I catch myself talking out loud to myself as I evaluate the hands I am dealt. (Without question, this habit needs breaking if I hope to be competitive and retain partners.)

Lest you be thinking that poker has more appeal than duplicate bridge, be advised the following.

> *Six retired Italian Floridian fellows were playing poker in the condo clubhouse when Guido loses $500 on a single hand, clutches his chest, and drops dead at the table. Showing respect for their fallen comrade, the other five continue playing, but standing up. At the end of the game, Giovanni looks around and asks, "So, who's going to tell his wife?"*
>
> *They cut the cards. Pasquale picks the lowest card and has to carry the news to Guido's widow. They tell him to be discreet, be gentle, try not to make a bad situation any worse.*
>
> *"Discreet? I'm the most discreet person you'll ever meet. Discretion is my middle name. Leave it to me!"*
>
> *So, Pasquale goes over to Guido's condo and knocks on the door. The wife answers through the door and asks what he wants. Pasquale declares: "Your husband just lost $500 in a poker game. He's afraid to come home."*
>
> *"Tell him to drop dead!" yells the wife. "I'll go tell him," says Pasquale.*

13

Heading for Hoover—the Sequel

My son-in-law also has ambitions to write a book. So he and I have, from time to time, exchanged ideas on the books we plan to write, as well as pointers on how to go about it. As such, he knows that I hate to write, he knows I am working on *Now What?*, and I guess he wants to "help." He also knows that one of the chapters I have planned is about stand-up comedy and that I can't apply the SCALES scale effectively unless I experience it. Just to make me feel more comfortable about my pending initiation into the field, he sends me an article he has just read in *The New York Times* entitled "Inside the Brutal World of Comedy Open Mikes."

The piece begins: "It takes a special kind of masochist to willingly endure the horrors of performing stand-up at New York City open mikes."[111] It then goes on to describe the author's single night trek to three different comedy clubs in New York watching one aspiring comic after another bomb in their erstwhile attempts to make patrons laugh. The humiliation of the aspiring comics described in the article is palpable.

The Times' portrayal of the world of beginners in comedy is not particularly uplifting news given that I have told my family that I have similar aspirations and that my research has shown that the most common way to jump in is through open-mike nights offered at most comedy clubs. (To be clear, my research has consisted of one, fairly lengthy, conversation with the son of a friend who graduated from an Ivy League college and then made his parents proud by moving to Chicago to pursue comedy. He now teaches second grade at a local public school, in part, because it is easier.) I suppose my son-in-law thinks that providing the article is a way to show support. Others could view it as the "s" in an S&M routine.

Having been warned by none other than *The New York Times*, I decide that rather than taking the plunge, I should put a toe in the water by first just watching. A quick Google search of the term "open-mike stand-up comedy" quickly establishes that the only regular such activity in the Birmingham area takes place each Friday night at The Stardome Comedy Club in Hoover, just about a mile as the crow flies from the Birmingham Duplicate Bridge Club where Queen Jean and Mike have ushered me into their world. Now that I know the quickest route to Hoover, it seems like it might be fun to check out a different scene there.

My wife and I arrive at The Stardome just before the 8:00 show is supposed to start. The smallish room is full but not crowded, with 40 people in attendance. No comedians take the stage for the first 30 minutes, but several waitresses work hard to make sure everyone (including the amateur jokesters) has plenty to drink. We are all well aware of the reverse correlation between inhibitions and alcohol intake.

Soon a Master of Ceremonies takes the stage and goes through a short, relatively funny routine to loosen up the crowd. After about 15 minutes of jokes, the emcee introduces a string of 10 or so acts, each lasting between five and 15 minutes. The acts contain widely varying material, causing reactions that range from guffaws to groans. The spectrum of talent is so wide that my wife and I reach the conclusion that some stand-up veterans have been sprinkled into the group, but it is hard to tell who are the amateurs and who are pros. Could be the litmus test is who has the dirtiest routines. The amateurs had to agree in advance not to use profanity. The host comedian was probably the best.

The winner of the informal polling of the crowd is Doobie Allen, a rotund twenty-something who talks about getting "whoopings" as a child (and who brings the most friends and family to The Stardome to cheer him on, including the parents who had administered the beatings). (All names have been changed to protect the comedians and their families.) Runner-up is Rick Johnson, a skinhead wannabe with a snide leer that he can morph into an effeminate smile. His jokes about being mistaken for being gay are the best part of his routine.

As we drive home, I can tell that my wife has serious misgivings about this whole comedy idea. She says it was like watching a train wreck. To her, it seems like some of the comedians resorted to crudity just to get a laugh (although she admits that the funniest joke of the night to her was also one of the crudest). She seems to be embarrassed for me and I haven't even bombed yet. For me, it has a) caused me to rethink my approach; and b) made me realize that preparation and coming up with a rock-solid routine is very, very important.

What about improv? Is that a comedic outlet that would be a good match for my personality? In this form of comedy, the emcee of the show solicits random ideas from the audience or describes impromptu situations for the comedians to run with. Obviously, the ability to think quickly on your feet is the principal skill set required here and preparation doesn't improve your improv's production of laughs from the audience.

The son of a friend has performed amateur improv at a club in Atlanta for several years. He practices law as an environmental lawyer during the day, but he and his wife perform improv on the weekends whenever they can. I reach out to him and get tickets to watch amateur improv one weekend at the Village Theater in Midtown Atlanta. My wife and I enjoy the show and find watching others deal with surprising challenges in a funny way as a great form of comedic entertainment.

I quickly determine, however, that I am not cut out for improv. My personality is not suited for rapid-fire interaction with others in ever-changing factual settings. I am tempted to give it a try but believe that the sacrifice of my self-esteem is better spread on the altar of a form of comedy that at least seems suited to my innate abilities. I would rather plan and practice and fail than simply stand onstage looking stupid.

So, I am faced with a dilemma. My humor does not seem to be suited to the audiences who frequent open-mike sessions. I'm so old that I'm almost always home drinking warm milk before many of the comedy venues open. My research indicates that this pursuit is very akin to self-flagellation. To top it all off, my loved ones think I'm nuts even to try this.

Then I have a revelation. What if I came up with a routine based on political humor from a conservative slant. I have often found some of the political analysis from the other side of the political spectrum to be riddled, from my point of view, with hypocrisy and irony. Why not add a little humor and try to work some of these ideas up into a comedy routine.

This idea gains some momentum with me when I hear a comment made during one of the first broadcasts of a new program on National Public Radio called "One A." On this day, the program consists of a panel of left-leaning comedians, talking about their profession. The program's host says that he wanted to include a conservative comedian but couldn't find one. I am somewhat doubtful that One A with its decidedly liberal leanings did a comprehensive search for a right-leaning comedian, but there does seem to be a dearth of funny folks coming at current issues with humor from a conservative viewpoint. Since I subscribe to the principle that nature abhors a vacuum, I decide it might be fun to take a stab at filling this void.

I reach out to a friend who serves as legal counsel to the Alabama Republican Party. He likes the idea and agrees to send me a list of Republican party officials around the state, mostly the chairs of the Republican executive committees in each of the counties. I recognize a few names on the list and reach out to a couple of the people I know in the more rural counties. My logic is that I may be able to try out a couple of routines in what would be the rural Alabama equivalent of the Poconos to a Vaudeville comedian. My calls to my contacts result in mild, but quizzical, encouragement. Unfortunately, by now we are into the early summer of a year with little electoral activity. The combination of summer vacations, the adjournment of the state legislature, and a lack of hard-fought campaigns means that the county committees, particularly outside of urban areas, have shifted into inactive status.

About this time, my life takes a detour—and not one that is suitable for a joke. All right…if you insist.

When the owners of a home in a well-to-do neighborhood packed up their car for an overnight trip, a burglar saw his big chance. He sneaked into the home, and it was everything he had hoped for—big-screen TV, stereo equipment, jewelry, and cash!

The burglar was literally dancing through the house with excitement when he heard a voice say "Jesus is watching you." Startled, the burglar turned off his flashlight and stood very still. When he heard nothing after a minute or two, he thought he must have imagined the voice. He turned on his light and went back to work.

As he unplugged the TV, he heard the voice again: "Jesus is watching you." This time he turned his light toward the voice, only to see a parrot in its cage. "Did you say that?" asked the burglar.

"Jesus is watching you," said the parrot.

"Stupid bird—what's your name?" asked the burglar.

"Moses" came the reply.

"What kind of fool names a parrot 'Moses'?" asked the now frustrated burglar.

The parrot looked at the burglar and said, "I guess the same kind of fool who names their Rottweiler 'Jesus'."

14

Heading for Hell (and Back)— Bookus Interruptus

Okay, so, things appear to be rocking along. I've started working on a comedy routine, and I have had some receptivity from some Alabama Republican county chairmen about giving my shtick a test drive. I've pretty much decided to steer away from Sacred Harp singing. Service clubs and duplicate bridge are maybes, and I have begun to make real progress committing the process to paper. Then, my own body decides to take me out of the game—at least for a while.

If the truth be known, one of the unspoken motivations for undertaking this whole process of trying to plan for a "life after career" was a problem I had with my back. For years, my back had become more and more of an impediment to my attempts to fully enjoy an active lifestyle. Surgical intervention over two years before had provided an enormous amount of relief. As I would say when friends asked for a post-surgery report: "I'm not 100%, but I'm 100% better." That response began to change about a year after the surgery as the discomfort gradually returned, first reappearing about the time of the Sacred Harp singing I joined in Tuscaloosa and growing gradually, but steadily, worse.

I have volumes of medical descriptions of what my back problem is, but the best description is the one provided by a fancy pants Washington, D.C., doctor when, after he had provided us with the formal medical explanation of my issues, was asked by my wife if he could provide a simpler description: "Yes ma'am. He has a 'bad back'." I will also spare you the long and drawn out process I undertook to try to find any solution to the problem short of surgery. Trust me—no less invasive fix seemed to work. Now that I am just over two years out from my first back operation, I have once again found myself unable to walk more than a couple hundred yards (even with my back brace) without having to sit down. The doctors tell me they think they can fix it (perhaps for good, this time); they just need to fuse five more vertebrae together and install two 9-inch-long, titanium rods in my lower back.

My memory of the post-surgery recuperative process from my last back operation, descriptions from friends of nightmarish back surgeries they have endured, my hope that other kinds of intervention might relieve the discomfort, and my desire to finish this book all combined to postpone the "big event." That hope begins to fade as I find that I am unable to stand in one spot for more than a couple minutes or walk the two blocks from my office to the weekly Downtown Rotary meetings without having to find a place to sit along the way. Nevertheless, with certain accommodations, I believe I am getting by.

Then, one morning I wake up after a fitful night's sleep and discover that my back has unilaterally declared a work stoppage. As my grandfather would have said, I am stove up. I have tremendous difficulty just getting out of bed. After several hours and several doses of the various medicines the docs have prescribed, I am able to function, but I realize that I am postponing the inevitable and call my doctor to schedule surgery.

The surgeon, however, is careful to set my expectations. He suggests that my previous surgery, which had been a mind-blowing experience from my standpoint, was a walk in the park compared to what I could expect with his proposed procedure. He says that I should plan to be out of commission for eight weeks and to expect the sustained level of discomfort to be significantly worse than the last surgery. No problem, I think. It reminds me of the punch line of one of my favorite Irish jokes, as paraphrased to apply here: "Eight weeks off, and a good reason to lose some weight." Also, a great opportunity to work on my book, right? Boy, was I misguided.

What I underestimate is the enormous effect that pain has on the ability to concentrate. Of course, there are ways to deal with the pain that comes along with the surgery—a.k.a. pain "killers." It turns out that those drugs don't really kill the pain, they just enable you to ignore it. Unfortunately, they also cause you to ignore everything else. You spend a lot of time just staring out the window thinking how nice it would be to open your laptop and write something brilliant. The trouble with that plan is that writing in this condition is much like trying to walk through hip-high mud—you can flail away, but real progress is very slow. Plus, you are lethargic when you are not asleep and you are asleep many more hours than at any time since you slept in a crib. All in all, not a formula for maximum productivity.

But—what a great time to put my research on resilience to the test! I reread my chapter on the subject and list out the elements for promoting resilience:

- Supportive social network—Back surgery could be the poster child for illustrating the importance of your friends and family to achieving a full and on-time recovery. I quickly realize how critical my wife is to making sure that I don't hurt myself during the period of maximum pain med dosage. (Fortunately, the only harm inflicted was economic. I made multiple purchases of the same items off of Amazon in the days after I was sent home from the hospital, not realizing that the prior purchases were on the way.) She also sees to it that all the meds are refilled and taken at the right time in the right dosages, that I eat despite a lack of appetite, that I manage to get in a shower occasionally, and that I am as comfortable as possible as I recuperate.

  My friends also go out of their ways to provide emotional support as well as reading materials and a lifetime supply of cookies, ice cream, and chicken salad. The more spiritually attuned members of my network also add me to their prayer list. Others check in with visits, both electronic and in-person, to monitor my progress. There is no way to overstate the importance of my social network to my recovery.

- Self-care habits—Over the first four weeks of my recovery, I lose 25 pounds. Given that my issues are skeletal, all of the docs advising me agree that less is good in this case, but some of the blood tests suggest that less intake of calories has also meant a little vitamin deficiency, resulting in more daily pill intake—a manageable problem.

  In terms of sleep, I probably go a little overboard, logging 10 to 14 hours of sleep every day for the first four weeks following surgery. I know this excess will need to change, but my docs encourage it. As the pain subsides and prescription meds play less of a role in my life, normal sleep patterns return.

Exercise, by all accounts, will be an essential factor in trying to increase the odds that I never have to do this again. In fact, I plan to use it as my first line of defense in fighting off the attacks from those 25 pounds as they try to reoccupy the territory they have lost. During the first eight weeks after the operation, however, I am put on a strict BLT regimen—I am not allowed to Bend, Lift, or Turn. For several weeks after that, I continue to be restricted to only those activities approved by my physical therapist. Gradually, I am able to add swimming, walking, and stretching back into the routine and lose the therapist. I commit to making regular exercise and core muscle control a surgery prevention partner.

- Meaning, purpose, and personal growth—As I emerge from the fog of pain control, I am able to recommit myself to the process of planning for my next few trips around the sun. Not only do my attempts at productivity provide some semblance of meaning and purpose, but they provide much-needed distraction from the diminishing, but still significant, discomfort from surgery. Clearly, there is little good that comes from ruminating on the aches and many advantages to trying to return to a more productive lifestyle. As the pain (and drugs) diminish, productive pursuits gradually replace mindless entertainment in the form of daytime TV, the laptop opens more and more, and I begin to pick back up where I left off on my writing, although I can't go back to applying my research to active pursuits just yet. About 11 weeks after surgery, I'm finally able to return to the bridge table for the first time.

- Spirituality—One advantage to the pain that comes along with back surgery is the glimpse that it gives you of what Hell must be like. One advantage to the pain drugs is the free flow and inward-looking thinking that comes along with staring into space for long periods of time. One advantage to the total reliance you have on your support network is the profound sense of gratitude that you have for those who care for you. Add it all up and I suppose I'm having a spiritual experience. I hope that I can translate this into a better, and longer lasting, understanding of the increasing importance that resilience will play going forward and integrate these elements in day-to-day activities after the surgery has faded into memory.

- Mental activity—I realize from the outset that meaningful mental activity and chemical pain control are mutually exclusive concepts. Unfortunately, in the weeks immediately following surgery, the pain levels were high enough that "mental activity" is the equivalent of "suffering," and pain pills are my friends. As time passes and healing progresses, the pain morphs into varying degrees of discomfort. At this point, the surgeon continues to mandate limited physical activity, so mental activity becomes an important distraction from the uncomfortable side effects of the procedure. Gradually, I am able to focus on writing, and getting into the flow it provides enables me to cut back more quickly on the pharma.

- Optimism—Throughout the process, the mantra that I keep repeating is that the surgery and the painfully slow recuperative process will be worth it—that the result will be the ability to more fully enjoy an active lifestyle. A turning point in the process is the day when I realize that, for a sizable portion of the day, I am experiencing less pain post-surgery than I was in the months leading up to surgery. This development is a tipping point and actually enables more optimism about what I can hope to achieve in the future. In my view, there is no way to get through an experience of this sort without optimism. In this case, the slow but (fairly) steady improvement in my condition made it relatively easy to have a bright outlook on my recovery and expectations for a better life.

Toward the end of six weeks of sequestration away from the office, I am able to return to work on a very part-time basis and to my research on my possible passions. After about eight weeks, I pass that tipping point where I inwardly declare the gain was worth the pain. Just shy of my eleven-week anniversary, I am released from physical therapy with instructions to continue to take it easy on physically demanding tasks. Gradually, my life returns to normal.

My unanticipated foray into testing my research on resilience continues, but early results seem to indicate that there is much benefit to be gained from following the rubric. The really compelling lesson from my back problems is that events such as this happen, they happen whether or not you try diligently to avoid them, and they don't happen on your schedule. More importantly, we can and should expect these episodes to occur more often as we age. All the more reason we need to equip ourselves with the necessary mental tools to deal with the trials and tribulations that we all will face sooner or later.

I am in no way suggesting that regular trips to the surgical wing of the hospital is a passion to pursue; no application of the SCALES scale is warranted here. The elements are, nevertheless, very similar—so similar in fact that I come away with the conclusion that using the SCALES approach to activities going forward will contribute to my resilience as I incur any future setbacks—challenges that are almost guaranteed to come if I live long enough. Another case of win/win for me and the SCALES approach.

And, by the way, I did manage to lose 25 pounds in the process. Now if I can just keep it off...

Which takes me back to that story about two Irish fellows.

> *Kennedy and O'Brien are going out for a night on the town and planning on getting into some trouble. O'Brien looks at Kennedy and says, "You should make a good confession before we go out tonight."*
>
> *Kennedy replies, "Not on me life. Father Murphy is in the confessional and you know how toof he is on penance." But O'Brien finally prevails, drives Kennedy to the Church and waits outside.*
>
> *Kennedy begins in the usual fashion: "Bless me, Father, for I have sinned. I have been sleepin' with a woman not of me household." Fr. Murphy replies, "In order for me to grant absolution, you are going to have to tell me who the woman t'is. Is it Mrs. Callahan who lives near the golf course?"*
>
> *Kennedy refuses to name the woman and says, "No, Father, tisn't and I am not going t' tell you who t'is." Fr. Murphy recognizes the sinner from*

his voice and asks, "Is that you, Kennedy?" Kennedy quickly replies, "No, Father, t'is not me and I'm not going to tell you who she is."

Fr. Murphy asks again, "Is it Mrs. O'Neil who lives in the center of town?" to which Kennedy replies, "No, Father, and I'm not going t' tell you her name."

Exasperated, Fr. Murphy says, "Kennedy, I'll give you one last chance and if you don't tell me who t'is I'm going to have to excommunicate you. Is it Mrs. Crowley who lives next to the Church?"

Kennedy responds, "No, Father, and I'm not going t' tell you!" At this point, the priest roars, "That's it. You're excommunicated for 30 days. Now, get out of m' Church!"

Kennedy returns to the waiting O'Brien, who asks, "So, how'd it go?"

Kennedy replies, "It went grand! I got me 30 days off and three good leads."

15

Heading for Hoover—the Sequel (continued)

When I took my side trip to explore the wonderful world of major back surgery, I thought I had charted a path that would lead to becoming the world's preeminent Republican stand-up comic. Then, a funny thing happens—the phone isn't ringing. All of the seeds I had planted don't seem to germinate. Once I emerge from my opioid cloud, I make a few calls and get the same kind of responses—pleasant agreement that the concept sounds inviting, but no hard and fast invitations to appear and try it out in person.

After several more whacks of my head against this wall, I decide to take a different tack. I may not have been comfortable trying to convert my humor to the kind of crowd that frequents most open-mike venues, but what if I tried to find a venue that would be suited to my kind of comedy. Of course, in a way that was what I had tried with little success with the Republican County Committees. But what if I could find an audience that is more suited to my humor, as opposed to trying to change my jokes to fit the audience. What about trying to laugh at my current stage of life: older American humor?

As I cast about for an opportunity to give stand-up a try, all signs point back to The Stardome Comedy Club in Hoover, where my wife and I had seen a fairly disorganized open-mike session months before. In my research, I learn that The Stardome has recently revamped its program to try to return it to a viable on-ramp for aspiring entrants into the world of professional comedy. The reincarnation is known as "The Colossal Comedy Side Show" and the new producer is Tim Spinosi.

Tim is a 53-year-old comedian with a miskempt salt-and-pepper beard and a long ponytail. He boasts of having been in the comedy trade for over 30 years. He also professes to have run several open-mike shows over the preceding two decades. He possesses an air of someone who has seen it all and done it all in the world of aspiring comics. He has revamped The Stardome's open-mike venue to being a real competition, with real judges and a real prize, in the form of a chance to perform on the Big Stage at The Stardome, where all the big-name comedians perform when they come to town and hundreds of people pay big money to hear the routines.

All of these developments cause my wheels to turn. What if I were to return to the Side Door stage at The Stardome for Tim's open-mike competition and try to populate the room with people who are roughly my age? I could then focus my jokes on the type of humor that appeals to truly more mature audiences. (Of course, one problem right out of the gate is that Tim's open-mike-night sessions start at 8:00 p.m.—a time slot that is starting to get a little late for some in my age group.)

At this point, I happen upon a stroke of good luck in the form of Joe Bean. Joe is a 25-year-old recent college graduate with an ambition to become a comedy writer. One of the holdbacks for Joe is that he has no real experience in stand-up, although he attended a good deal of live comedy and has participated in some improv shows. I hear from a friend that Joe is looking for involvement in the Birmingham comedy scene, so I call him and enlist his help in refining my routine. He agrees to help.

After my initial meeting with Joe this approach appeals even more to me. Joe has a great sense of humor and is just starting out too. I figure I can get great pointers on jokes and he can gain some much-needed experience in writing comedy and managing egos by working with me. Also, Joe has recently been hired by The Stardome as a waiter. Based on my research, this is a fairly standard point of entry for fledgling comedians. Whether or not he can use the waiter job to vault into a writing slot for others, I am thinking he can share valuable inside knowledge of the inner workings of the venue. Finally, since Joe's credentials as a millennial are impeccable, he may be able to sand the rough edges off of my "insights on aging" routine to make it more humorous for the younger set.

I draft a routine that is a tongue-in-cheek speech on the signs of approaching old age and the ups and downs of such a condition. Joe reviews it and gives invaluable feedback, as well as a few funny zingers based on his observations of his parents. He also points out the need to find some hooks, and some suggested additions, to draw in the younger crowd.

Joe and I go through a few more iterations of draft-review-redraft-review-refine on my material. I perform pieces of my routine for him to get his reaction. I buy the beer, and he provides the advice, some of which consists of glimpses into the inner workings of The Stardome. Perhaps his most valuable service is to provide the reinforcement that I need to hear that my new approach to this project is not completely nuts, and I'm not completely off my rocker.

Further research on stand-up produces an oft-repeated refrain about how every comedian bombs on his or her first few times on stage. As Amy Schumer puts it: "There's nothing quite like your first bomb. You can feel it in your bones. First you think there might be something wrong with the sound. But there isn't. It's you. You're the problem. You and your terrible jokes that are not funny."[112] Of course, there are a host of causes for bombing (although funny jokes are pretty damned important). First and foremost, everyone has a different sense of humor and what may seem quite witty to the writer may not strike a chord with the hearer. The joke just may not translate well to a particular audience on a given night.

In addition, delivery is key. You may have the funniest joke known to man, but if you fail to present the joke (and, more importantly, the punchline) in the right way, you won't achieve the desired result. Successful comedians cite timing as a critical element to producing laughter. In addition, voice volume, clarity, and speed of delivery are important to a great routine. Combining all of these elements into a cohesive, seemingly natural dialogue, of course, is the real trick, and it ain't easy. Jerry Seinfeld once put it this way: "[T]here will always only be a few great comedians because comedy itself is so difficult. No matter how many people do it, it's just a rare combination of skills and talents that go into making a great comedian."[113]

Because all of these rules are much easier to understand in the abstract than to apply in real time, I quickly come to the conclusion that several trial runs on willing guinea pigs are important steps in my process. After multiple revisions to my written routine and several mental practice runs, I give it a formal informal dry run over wet cocktails with my wife and two other couples who are close friends, roughly our same age. Despite their efforts to be gentle with my feelings, I can tell that I have much work to do.

Their reactions to my lines and their suggestions lead to further refinements of the routine and several changes in delivery. One of my biggest challenges is that I am supposed to limit my routine at The Stardome to five minutes. My private performance comes in at over double the allotted time despite one of the constructive criticisms being that I am talking much too fast. Cutting material that has taken so much effort to develop is difficult—a distant cousin of putting a much loved dog to sleep. I am still a month shy of my date at The Stardome, so I have plenty of time to work on it.

I chop, and I refine, and I reword, and I rework. My mini-performance makes me realize how age-specific my routine is. This conclusion causes me to become even more concerned that the typical youngish audience at The Stardome might not be very receptive to this genre of humor, and this realization causes me to come out of the closet with my close friends in the hopes that I can pack the house with older, friendlier faces. I let a group of them know when and where I will be performing my first public stand-up comedy routine. Shock, dismay, encouragement, and disgust ensue, but seven or eight couples declare their plans to attend.

An upcoming, long-planned family reunion provides a convenient venue for another trial run. My captive audience consists of about 28 people ranging in age from 11 to 71, with around a dozen over the age of 50. I am hopeful that the conditions are reasonably close to what I will find at the comedy club. There are close family members in attendance, but a good many that I see only rarely. Attendees are mostly Southerners, but some have come from as far away as California and Virginia. Also in attendance are a smattering of invited guests, mostly old family friends. All have agreed to offer up suggestions and constructive criticism following my performance. In addition, since I will perform after dinner, my audience will have had the opportunity to enjoy a happy hour and, if they chose, a little wine with dinner. Thus, the atmosphere should resemble that at an 8:00 open-mike session at The Stardome.

As soon as the dinner dishes are cleared, my brother-in-law silences the room and I give it my best shot, producing a good number of belly laughs—and a few blank stares. When the group provides feedback, I am struck by how varied the responses are. A joke that seems hilarious to one relative falls flat with another. As expected, my focus on the ramifications of aging means that my jokes have their desired impact mostly on the older members of the audience. There are a couple of jokes that seem to have universal appeal within the group, and some that have the opposite effect on all (and must be sent forthwith to rot in the circular file), but laughter production of most of the material seems to be subject to each recipient's particular sense of humor.

Upon reflection, I realize that this is the living, breathing manifestation of a principle I have heard about and read about—audiences are fickle, and even the best material will sometimes founder. One thread (at least with my family) is that the more off-color the joke, the better the reception. I also come to realize how important my delivery is to the success of the performance. And, despite my best efforts, I have been able to reduce my routine only to eight minutes. I discern from the comments, however, that my cadence has improved. With the help of a video that a nephew has taken of my performance, I go back to the drawing board with my material and try to cull the losers, rework the winners, and streamline the whole thing.

I now have a week to practice before my first public appearance and, as the big day approaches, I am surprisingly nervous. To add to the ominous air, I am scheduled for the show on Friday the Thirteenth (of October). My wife, who conveniently has plans to be out of town and can not attend, seems to believe that the date is somehow ratification of her absence.

A few days before we are set to perform, Tim sends out an open letter to the aspiring comedians who are scheduled for bad luck Friday and encourages us to work this coincidence into our acts. The letter also gives some history of The Stardome and the origins of "Side Show" as a moniker for his open-mike contest. According to Tim, during the golden age of the circus, each such venue would have its main activities under the Big Top, but there would always be other entertainment at adjacent tents, or "sideshows."

The sideshows typically had two formats: freak shows and burlesque. His letter continues: "Burlesque shows were basically stripper venues. But in between the striptease acts, guys would come up and tell jokes. This was the true birthplace of stand-up." Ergo, the "Side Show Stage" in Hoover—no burlesque, but some burly comics. (As an aside, Jay Leno says that when he started in the early Seventies, there were still not many venues around devoted to stand-up. As a result, he got his start doing his routines in strip joints.)[114]

Tim's letter also recounts that several famous comedians, including Steve Harvey, Sinbad, and Roy Woods, Jr., got their start at The Stardome and, by implication, I can too. The letter makes several general suggestions: Be your best, practice hard in advance, feel free to be theatrical, never stop being silly, and dress professionally. "Show up to my show wearing shorts and flip-flops and I'll bounce you out of here." (As it turns out, shorts would have been a step up from the attire adorning some of the comedians on the nights that I attend Tim's open-mike nights. There are no clown suits, but several outfits are equally as outlandish.)

Soon the primary purpose of the letter becomes clear: "Comedy is a business." Because you hope to make a living at it, and so do Tim and the owners of The Stardome, you need to develop your audience. The practical application of that principle for the Side Show is that you must bring at least four paying audience members with you. (In the business, I learn later, shows with such requirements are known as "Bringers.") He even provides PDFs of flyers you can use to promote the show with your friends and neighbors. He follows the marketing pitch with a reminder that a group of three judges will crown the evening's funniest comedian at the end of the night. The winning comic automatically goes on to the "grand finale" competition on the main stage of The Stardome in January. He implies that the more friends you have in the audience laughing uproariously at your jokes, the more likely the vote will go your way.

Even before I receive Tim's letter, I am glad that I have been recruiting a group of my friends to come to hear my routine. Candidly, my self-promotion is not driven by a desire to make it to the grand finale. I remember the average age of the audience from my trip to The Stardome as an observer and know that I need older people in the audience to have any chance of getting a chuckle.

All along my plan has been to direct my jokes at "more mature" members of the audience, and my trial runs have proved the wisdom of that conclusion—much of my humor is lost on millennials. As Jay Leno once put it: "The whole thing to do in comedy is finding a common bond with the people in the audience."[115] In other words, the likelihood of my falling flat is inversely correlated with the amount of gray hair in the audience.

A corollary of this condition is that the overall format of the show is crafted for hard-charging, hard-drinking, Friday night fun-seeking young people. Thus, the first act won't start until well after 8:00 p.m. and the last act is not likely to finish before 10:30 p.m. As a result, there is no way my crowd will stay long enough to hear the judges' verdict anyway. In fact, I have a tactical need to make sure that my five-minute slot on the agenda is early enough to capture the oldsters I am inviting before the sandman gets them.

Throughout the week leading up to my performance I focus on refining my routine to fit within the five minutes allotted and to committing the resulting act to memory. My wife catches me a couple of times walking around the yard outside, mouthing my lines quietly to myself. She encourages me to take my practice indoors lest the neighbors start questioning my mental stability. I tell her to leave the funny lines to me, but I take my practice sessions to the backyard anyway, just in case.

As Friday the Thirteenth approaches, I am somewhat surprised at my heightened level of anxiety and nerves. Over the years, my business, government, and civic roles have required significant amounts of public speaking, and I have always prided myself on not falling prey to the nervousness that undoes those who fear such opportunities. What is it about performing stand-up comedy that gives me the jitters? Why does the prospect of falling flat in front of 50 mostly inebriated patrons of The Stardome make me more nervous than speaking to 2,500 mortgage bankers at the opening of an annual convention? I conclude that the answer to these questions is rooted in the novelty of the situation and the dire reports of those who have gone before and who, after delivering their best joke, hear nothing but breathing from the audience. In the back of my mind I know that the evidence of my failure at the Side Show stage would be immediate, irrefutable, and irretrievable.

On the night of my performance I head to The Stardome early as instructed by Tim. My costume for the night is much like it would be on any Friday night. Since my monologue addresses the issues associated with aging, I am dressed like a 60-year-old yuppie. Tim points me to the sign-up list, and I grab the #5 slot. (Because no one takes the #1 slot, and the #2 comedian gets cold feet and removes his name from the list at the last minute, I move up to being the third amateur to appear.) I then calm my nerves by watching college football in the bar while the rest of the comics slowly assemble.

About 30 minutes before the Side Show is scheduled to commence, Tim calls everybody together for a pre-performance cast meeting to go over the rules and pump us all up, once again stressing that "comedy is a business." He goes through the list of what he considers taboo profanity—the "n" word, the "c" word, the "f" word, and "gd." Fortunately for several of the upcoming acts, he has not prohibited the "p" or "v" words. He describes the timer signal, a makeshift traffic signal, that will inform us that we have four minutes remaining (green), one minute remaining (yellow), and it's time to quit (red). His assistant describes the consequences of exceeding our allotted time (disqualification from possible participation in the grand finale) and asks us if we have any requests for the music that will be played as we walk to the stage. This final request bears a striking figurative resemblance to "What do you want for your last meal before we execute you?"

For the next half hour, the whole group mills around nervously, trying to make small talk with each other and occasionally glancing at whatever mnemonic devices we are using as cheaters for our routines. (In my case, it is a 3x5 index card. Others use iPhones, old-fashioned notebooks, or word processor printouts. One woman has listed her jokes on the back of her fist.) I spend most of this time visiting with my dozen or so friends who have assembled. I make sure no thirsts for adult beverages are unquenched. Once again, my interest in bar sales is less about the business of comedy and more about making sure my friends have the right frame of mind to laugh at my jokes.

At roughly 8:15, Tim starts the proceedings. He welcomes the crowd and introduces KJ, our emcee. (Once again, all names, other than Tim's, are fabricated.) KJ has an opening routine to get the crowd warmed up. Another pro, operating under the guise of being a newbie, Laurie, has wandered over from the Big Stage and follows KJ with a five-minute routine to further rev up the audience. And then the raw amateurs, one by one, take the stage and try our hands at the elusive art of stand-up comedy.

Counting me, there are now about 11 cows lined up for the slaughter. (The number keeps changing because people seem to keep striking their names from the list, and new names appear even after the program starts.) The demographic breakdown is roughly half male and half female. Likewise, the group is about 50/50, black/white. The vast majority of the group seems to be 20- and 30-year-olds, with me appearing to be the oldest participant by far. (Perhaps there is a message in this fact.)

As the group waits backstage to take turns at the mike, the scene reminds me of a movie of paratroopers in the dimly lit belly of a transport plane on their way to a battlefield. The atmosphere is tense, with nervous chatter, adrenaline, and repetitious referral to props, making sure that each laugh weapon is loaded with the best live ammo at his/her disposal. One by one each of the laughter soldiers exits the chamber onto the stage to do battle.

The two acts before me set fairly low bars. Each has a couple of jokes that are mildly amusing, but no barn burners. The audience is polite but in no way generous with its chortles. Both performers are clearly ill at ease and suffering from dire cases of the jitters. In a weird way, their discomfort raises my confidence level. One of the two, a woman, hits on a subject that will be a recurring theme throughout the night—women's crotches. Tim's neglect in not putting the "v" word and the "p" word off-limits is put to the test. The comic doesn't get the hook, but also doesn't get a laugh. Succeeding comics don't get the message and continue to focus with little comic success on that subject.

By about 9:00, my turn comes and I take the stage. My routine, as practiced, is focused on the subject of advancing age—its signs, drawbacks, and advantages. The audience, particularly the portion that is there because of my invitation and encouragement to liquor up, seems to find some humor in this topic, but I witness no one doubled over in laughter from my descriptions. I am pleased to notice that the few other patrons with a smattering of gray hair find my jokes funny. My routine stands out for the absence of any mention of female genitalia, unless you count a fleeting veiled reference to menopause.

I manage to make it through my performance without having to pull out my cheater card. (After the fact, I determine that I forgot only one of my jokes. Unfortunately, it is one of my better ones.) To my dismay, the yellow light, signifying only 60 seconds of my allotted time remaining, seems to light up as soon as I get started, despite the fact that I have pared down and polished my routine to its essence. As a result, my last three jokes are delivered at a breakneck clip, I thank the audience, and exit stage right.

The rest of the evening is spent listening to the remaining acts and thanking my friends who showed up as they gradually slip out as the night progresses, two-by-two falling prey to a long workday. I make it through the last performance and find that the crowd is harder to please the later it gets.

When all is said and done, only one of the acts all night is particularly noteworthy in its laughter-producing effect on the audience. The comedian is a young black guy named Morris in a referee shirt. His jokes are funny enough that it is difficult to determine if he is truly one of us or has been planted by Tim to juice up the performance. When Tim announces the judges' pick, Morris takes home the gold medal for the night, providing some confirmation that he is an amateur and that talent prevails at the Side Show.

Leaving The Stardome, I am comfortable that I did a credible job at my virgin performance as a stand-up comedian. My fear of hearing crickets was misfounded, in part because I had prepared, in part because I had subjected a couple of smaller, friendlier audiences to trial runs, and in part because I had made sure the Friday the Thirteenth audience included a big slug of close friends. I am proud of the fact that my routine didn't attempt to garner laughs through what I would consider raunchy or shock humor (although a couple of my jokes might have deserved an R rating).

By the next day, as I reflect on the evening, I am struck by how much I enjoyed the experience, as well as recurring thoughts about what I could have done better. I am reminded of an assessment of Harold Ramis (of *Ghostbusters* fame) about the successful performance of stand-up: "I've been onstage. I know what it feels like to have those waves of laughter. It's like being bathed in love. Once you've had it, it's like a drug. It wears off, and then you need something more."[116]

My next-day reflections also include a dose of remorse. I am *kicking* myself for not hanging around to mingle with some of my fellow rookies. I am also mildly looking forward to giving it "one more try." To that end, I reach out to Tim and confirm a date for my next appearance. Inwardly, I'm surprised that I harbor some illogical disappointment that there had been no hue and cry for my return to the stage. Could this be some variant or early symptom of the stand-up bug?

To improve my routine, I decide to seek some professional advice and I call Keith Cromwell, the executive director of the Red Mountain Theater. Keith has been an actor and director of live theater for over 30 years. He has appeared on Broadway and has acted in both drama and comedy over the years. More importantly, he has taught acting for decades, including to novices as young as their early teens. One of my friends had taken a bootleg video of my maiden performance at The Stardome, and I send it to Keith to critique my performance in the hopes he can help me increase my guffaw ratio.

Keith is very encouraging and goes out of his way to recognize that taking to the stage, particularly at my age, is not a comfortable role. After commending my courage (or maybe recklessness), he offers up several helpful and insightful suggestions, ranging from changes to my monologue to draw in the audience to ways to make the punchlines of my jokes more powerful. Naturally, Keith also emphasizes the importance of practice and hard work to perfect the delivery and timing and, ironically, to make it look easy and natural. He offers to allow me to practice my shtick in front of his class of high school students to get used to performing in front of an audience that won't even crack a smile at my jokes. I decline. Some embarrassments are simply too intolerable.

Back to the drawing board and bathroom mirror for practice. I redraft my routine (again), both to take Keith's pointers into account and to improve and tighten it. My Friday the Thirteenth performance exceeded the five-minute time limit by more than a minute despite my previous best efforts to cull. More importantly, by my own observation and Keith's coaching, I rushed through the material and failed to pause for effect after delivering punchlines. I resolve to be brutal in trimming the number of jokes to cover. (As I have gone through this process, I have saved the extracted material in a "parking lot" in case I ever want to revisit those ideas. My parking lot is now three times as long as my routine.)

My return trip to the Side Show stage at The Stardome is in many ways a repeat of my first with a few noticeable differences. The biggest surprise, for some reason that Tim and team can't explain, is the size of the audience. The crowd is substantially larger than at my previous outing. Management is able to squeeze a few more than 100 patrons into the room but has to turn some latecomers away at the door. I have managed to convince 12 uninitiated friends (plus my wife this time) to come out to Hoover for my encore, and I become concerned that some of the stragglers will not get a seat. We manage to slip every one of my guests into the room, but most are seated so far to the front that they can touch the stage, not an enviable place when a hungry comic starts looking for a gullible member of the audience to pick on.

Another notable difference is that the owner of The Stardome, Bruce Ayers, gives the pre-game pep talk before we start (and hangs around to watch a few of the acts). In his speech, he covers much of the same material as Tim at the Friday the Thirteenth performance, but his testimony about the path to fame and fortune starting at the Side Stage seems to carry more credibility. He states emphatically, "I can make it happen if you have the talent." He also gives a much more heartfelt pitch about the importance of ticket sales to the viability of our comedic careers. After revving the troops for about 15 minutes, he turns it back over to Tim to go through the obligatory reading of the rules.

At some point during the meeting, Bruce asks for a show of hands of first-timers and only one hand goes up (a guy who later appears to be dead drunk, leading to suspicion that this is part of his act). The next show of hands asks for out-of-towners. Most of the people in the room raise their hands. It turns out that only four or five of the performers are from the Birmingham area. This fact surprises me and I zero in on one of those who indicated that he was from out of town—a youngish guy with a red felt stocking cap and a colorful holiday tie who goes by the stage name—yep, you guessed it—Santa.

Santa tells me that he is a kitchen appliance salesman by day and a comic by night. (Later, it slips out that he sells Cutco knives door-to-door.) He tells me that he hails from Atlanta, Georgia, and that he has been working at becoming a comic for five years. Tonight will be his third open-mike performance of the week. After learning that this is only my second time out ever, he offers encouragement that, with perseverance, I can get to his level of success. At that point, he shows me an e-mail he has received that afternoon from someone wanting to pay him $75 to perform his routine. I congratulate him and tell him how much I look forward to hearing him on stage in a few minutes, but I am thinking that the amount promised seems to be a paltry sum to hire live entertainment. After seeing his performance on the Side Stage, I decide his client is overpaying.

Another important differentiating factor on this night (and a driver of the crowd size, I am sure) is the big turnout of aspiring comedians. When the curtain goes up, there are 15 wannabes lined up backstage to take their turns at the mike. Overall, it is a pretty diverse group of competitors—maybe slightly more black and male than the last time—and generally more talented than Friday the Thirteenth comics. Of the 15 performers, four or five are really pretty funny. A few others have one or two memorable lines. One is so drunk or stoned that some of my friends seated near the stage are concerned for their safety.

My turn at the mike comes early in the evening. By the time I sign up the earliest available slot is #11, but I ask Tim to move my name to an earlier slot if one becomes available, in case my team wants to check out after my gig. The next thing I know, I am in the #1 slot, immediately after Tim and the emcee warm up the crowd. I learn an important lesson from this: The crowd has high expectations of the lead-off batter on open-mike night.

The three funniest comics of the night in the view of the judges, and an informal poll of my friend group, are all black, two men and a woman. The winner of the three by the judge's tally is a younger guy whose routine is somewhat rambling and a bit political, but funny. My friends would have reversed the order and crowned Queen LaLaugha, a very large woman with a booming voice, as the funniest of the night title. After the show, I hear her say that she had won the competition a few weeks before. That fact makes me suspicious that the judges have put a thumb on the scales to ensure that the final competition in January includes a broad range of participants. (If there were one, I am certain that I would have won the prize for funniest in the Over 60 White Male category since I was the only participant who could qualify.)

At the end of the night, I feel reasonably good about my performance. I was more relaxed than before, and I remembered all of my jokes. I believe my delivery has improved, with a slower cadence and more pauses for effect. Per the instructions I received from Keith, I concentrated on individual members of the audience as targets for each joke rather than "machine-gunning" the crowd. My friends, none of whom think I was the best of the night, all found my performance to be in the small group of credibly funny acts of the night. All in all, I think it went well—until the ride home from Hoover.

My wife is unusually reticent in the car. When I ask her how she enjoyed the evening, she mentions the crowd, the room temperature, her front and center seat, the large number of acts, and the intoxicated young comedian—but no mention of my performance. After I press her, she reluctantly opines that I shouldn't have gone first and I should have made better use of the microphone. Clearly a slow learner, I press her some more and learn that she thinks I am "brave and interesting." These may be appropriate accolades for a Syrian Civil War news correspondent, but not the affirmation sought by an aspiring comedian. The adjective "funny" gets no mention in her assessment.

Slowly, it sinks in that one of the traits of many of the comics I have seen in the various open-mike sessions that I have attended or in which I have participated is self-delusion. Bruce and Tim may be able to cite examples of comics who failed to hit their comedic strides until after enduring several years of embarrassing effort, but there are many more who lack some basic ingredient for making it on stage. In many ways, it reminds me of the advice my banjo teacher gave me years before in a brief counseling session following a couple of years of lessons: "Rob, you may always enjoy plucking your banjo, but you're never going to be any good." I believe my wife had just rendered the same judgment in a nicer way about my future in stand-up. I may be able to provide entertainment at cocktail parties, but don't sit by the phone waiting for Saturday Night Live to call.

Having given it the good old college try, it is now time to turn the tables on comedy and see how it rates as a possible pursuit on the SCALES scale.

Social Interaction—No question that my foray into this field has caused me to get way out of my comfort zone, meeting a new group of people from different walks of life and largely from a different age group than the one with which I normally hang. I think it is safe to say that, even though The Stardome and the

Birmingham Duplicate Bridge Club are within shouting distance of each other in Hoover, I did not bump into a single person who frequents both. In a weird way, however, the regulars in both buildings have some similarities.

There is a small group at the BDBC that teaches the lessons, makes the rules, and provides the directors of the matches. At The Stardome, there is a small group of people, like Tim, who have been around for years, coaching the newbies, running the sound and lights, and performing warm-up routines for the visiting (or brand new) comics. In both settings, the regulars form a sort of family.

The analogy seems to break down after that. Duplicate bridge players, service club members, and Sacred Harp singers all seem to develop social networks with the other rank-and-file participants. Comics don't seem to enjoy the same benefits from their activity. My experience is that there is a bit of bonding with your fellow actors on the night of the performance, but the relationships don't extend beyond that night. In part, this may be a result of the fairly itinerant nature of the group, traveling from one open-mike opportunity to another with different casts showing up at each.

This condition doesn't improve as the comic climbs the ladder of success. When I first started examining the field, I interviewed a young schoolteacher named Kent Haines. Kent had dreamed of being a stand-up comic from an early age and had decided to pursue his dream. He started with the painful process of open-mike performances in Philadelphia, Pennsylvania. Over time he was successful and won a competition that led to a spot on Comedy Central. There, through a combination of hard work and talent, he made a name for himself then moved to Chicago and started lining up paying gigs. Success at that level led to an opportunity to go on the road being hired to perform at various venues around the country. It was while reaching for this brass ring that Kent underwent an epiphany.

While sitting in a hotel room in Portland, Oregon, waiting to perform that night, Kent realized that he had chosen a very lonely profession. He also realized that the more successful he became, the lonelier it would get. Soon thereafter, he returned home to Alabama, became a schoolteacher, and started a family. Kent's experience with comedy suggests my limited assessments of the social interactions aren't far off the mark and likely wouldn't improve with more exposure to the pastime.

In a bizarre way my foray into the world of stand-up may have had more of a relationship-enhancing effect on my everyday interactions with my regular group of friends. When word got out of my harebrained efforts to try comedy, my long-standing friends were intrigued. The reaction from my family and friends ranged from dismay (my wife) to curiosity to downright encouragement. I believe it is safe to say that many people harbor a secret desire to try comedy, but are worried that such efforts somehow may be interpreted as a sign of excess frivolity or mental instability. At the least, most folks are curious about what it must be like backstage with such apparently zany, offbeat characters. I have had, as a result, a host of conversations with the unlikeliest acquaintances about my experience in the world of comedy. My closest friends and family—those who know me the best—just seem to shake their heads and mutter "What next?"

Taking all this into account and despite the icebreaking aspects at cocktail parties of a reputation as a comic, a score of four seems appropriate.

Concentration—It would be easy, upon reflection on my short career in comedy, to believe that any activity that occurs in intervals measured only in weeks and months cannot involve sustained levels of concentration. Wrong.

First, I was surprised by how much thought it takes to come up with a really funny joke. There can be no question that delivery is critical, but my experience at The Stardome taught me the fundamental truth that the base ingredient in any routine is the jokes. Preparing to perform taught me the difficulty of composing the jokes. Turning a humorous thought into a line that will convey the humor is tough, even to make it funny to yourself. To transform that concept into something that a broader audience will understand and be amused by is enormously tricky.

After my fateful performances at The Stardome, I spent some time studying the science behind comedy and the elements that are commonly found in funny material. (You are probably wondering, logically, why I didn't do this research before I went on stage. I don't have a good answer.) You can read in *Psychology Today* how there may be a "neural circuit in the brain that responds exclusively to laughter."[117] The expert teachers in the field can instruct you in using setup and punchlines to create expectation and surprise. You can also learn basic concepts of economy, common knowledge, revelation, using hard consonants to make words funnier, and the rule of threes (as in three examples, participants, or subjects in each joke).[118] And the list goes on and on, and the complexity increases.

There may be science, but it really boils down to talent and hard work. At a more basic level, all instructors (including Tim Spinosi of Side Stage fame) encourage you to fall back on those issues that seem funny to you. Each recommends that you carry a journal with you at all times to jot down those humorous thoughts that come to you at the oddest of times. When you next go back to revising your routine or drafting a new one, you should pull out your notebook, apply all rules that you have learned, and flesh out the humorous thought to see if it can morph into a laugh-producing joke.

The point here is that the work involved to be a comedian requires much more thought and time than I ever imagined when I started my foray into stand-up. Talent, science, and structure are important at some level, but good old-fashioned work is a central ingredient that every comic will return to as a critical key to success. Moreover, the funnier and smoother the routine, the more work and thought has been invested in it.

Additionally, you can write the funniest routine imaginable, and if you don't manage to remember the punchlines, you are in trouble. I learned that even a five-minute routine takes enormous concentration to remember the jokes, with the right punchlines, in the right order for maximum effect. On top of remembering the material, the finer points of delivery require focus and practice. My time working with Keith Cromwell impressed upon me the importance of eye contact, speed of delivery, and timing. Trying to get all of these elements to mesh and to do so in a manner that doesn't seem contrived is much more difficult than I would have thought. It has forever changed the way that I watch, and appreciate, great comedians.

A reader who has never tried to be funny in front of a crowd of people may think I am overly generous here, but I believe stand-up deserves a score of eight on this element.

Accomplishment—For some reason, my brief foray into stand-up—when it connected—provided me an enormous sense of accomplishment. Somehow, much like writing, there is a sense of having produced a product. Better than writing, you are able to gauge success immediately by the size of the guffaw.

Continuing the analogy to writing, when trying to come up with the best routine, rewriting and refinement are critical. Even after you've come up with a well-connected set of jokes, endless edits and reworks follow each performance as you try to perfect your material. Much like duplicate bridge, there seem to be unlimited opportunities in the field requiring ever-increasing skill levels and there is plenty of competition at each step. Instead of accumulating masterpoints, though, your gauge of success is based on being funny enough to garner invitations to perform and, ultimately, finding someone willing to pay you for your efforts. I suppose there is some pinnacle that one reaches if you are a Steve Martin or Carol Burnett, but given the age at which I am starting, let's just say I'm not worried about hitting the ceiling.

It is important to realize that there are some attendant risks to chasing comedy as a dream. There is the reputation risk from pursuing an endeavor that is perceived as less than serious. In my view, this is really just a perception problem, rather than a real problem, because of the difficulty of the pursuit.

You also have to realize that the accomplishment (and the social interaction) often take place in an environment that your mother would not find to be "wholesome." By and large, if you follow the traditional route to success in stand-up comedy, you are performing late at night in front of people who you kinda, sorta hope have made your job easier by altering their own state of consciousness, usually through the consumption of plenty of alcohol. Oddly, it is the adrenaline that courses from making these people laugh that keeps you alert in this setting long past your own bedtime. (At least you could tell your mother that the rooms are no longer smoke filled—unless, of course, you get a gig in one of the states where the recreational use of cannabis is legal.)

Add it all together and the accomplishment I felt from performing comedy, even though any tangible evidence of accomplishment eludes me, is fairly high. I assign it a score of seven.

Laughter—Stop, you're killing me. Ten.

Exercise—Not much here. At least I took to practicing my routines while walking (briskly) around the yard. I notice that some of the other comedians exhibited a good deal of frenetic energy onstage. Not me. After all, the themes of my skit are the risks and rewards of getting old. Too much energy spoils the mood. Perhaps I've hit on an idea—require the audience to circle the stage while doing deep knee bends while I tell jokes "in the round" and add an element of prevention to my act.

Until then, my observation is that whatever physical activity occurs, there is very little aerobics to it. If you are successful with your routine, you may send your audience into convulsions of laughter, but that doesn't provide you, the actor, much of a cardio workout.

Once again, comedy as a serious pursuit requires getting out of the house (although, based on my observation of the other open-mike comics at The Stardome, not necessarily out of your pajamas). As a result, I'll be generous and give it a two.

Spirituality—Another no-show, unless you ascribe some points for helping others get their daily dose of chuckles or the prayers offered up before going onstage to fend off mortal embarrassment. Surely, there is a field of religious humor that could allow you to garner some spirituality points, but it is largely absent from the comedy venues that I have seen. (I suppose it should be stated for the record that the preachers of my favorite sermons in church always seem to find a way to weave in some humor, but I didn't run into many clergy at The Stardome.) Stand-up gets a score of only one here.

Plug all of these scores into the matrix and you arrive at a composite score of 6.4. After feeding my assessments into the spreadsheet and reading the overall score, I was surprised to see how low it was. Throughout my efforts to give comedy a run for its money, the state of flow came easily. I felt challenged and absorbed in applying my skill sets to a new field. When writing, revising, practicing, or performing my routines, whether directed at the Republican faithful or folks trying to find humor in growing older, I lost track of the time and my surroundings. This disconnect may indicate a flaw in the SCALES process, or an indicator that it works in ferreting out activities that seem to be enjoyable but objectively need assignment to life's been-there-done-that bin of obscurity. You be the judge.

By now, it should come as no surprise to you that my routine focused on some of the frustrations and indignities that arise as you grow older, such as when two old friends meet again.

A woman was sitting in the lobby waiting to be called for her first appointment with a new dentist. She noticed his dentistry diploma on the wall, which bore his full name.

Suddenly, she remembered a tall, handsome, dark-haired boy with the same name who had been in her high school class some 40-odd years ago. Could he be the same guy she had had a secret crush on, way back then?

Upon seeing him, however, she quickly discarded any such thought. This balding, gray-haired man with the deeply lined face was way too old to have been her classmate.

After he examined her teeth, she asked him if he had attended Red Bluff High School. "Yes. Yes, I did. I'm a Spartan," he said, gleaming with pride.

"When did you graduate?" she asked.

He answered, "In 1978. Why do you ask?"

"You were in my class!" she exclaimed.

He looked at her closely. Then she heard the ugly, old, wrinkled son-of-a-bitch ask...

"What did you teach?"

16

Heading for Hemingway's House

So, the suspense is over and the secret is out. As I work through several of the possible paths to take for the next five/ten/twenty years, one of the candidates on my list is to take up nonfiction writing as a serious pastime. What better way to test-drive that idea, and evaluate it purposefully, than to write a book on the "possible paths to take" in retirement, huh? In a sense, you are my guinea pig on this one. Many thanks for your help. I owe you a beer.

Without question, the title of this chapter is a fraud. I am no Hemingway on any number of levels, not the least of which is the inadequacy of my imagination to write fiction. I am under no illusion that now I just need to sit by the phone and wait for the call from the Pulitzer Committee. Nevertheless, having the ability and desire to string together understandable sentences to describe my undertakings has given me the structure I need. Having the overall project of committing the results of my research to writing also had the effect of bringing some discipline to my efforts. Without the goal of completing a book comprising my ideas, my experiences, and the results, no doubt procrastination would have taken control of the effort long before now. After all, it has taken over two years to complete the process as it is.

Where did that time go? It may not be apparent from what you've read here, but this project has required a fair amount of the "library" kind of research as I have read up on the broad range of topics I have covered in developing and applying the SCALES scale. Even more time-consuming was the legwork to try out the various possible passions. The actual writing occupied many early mornings, as I attempted to stick to a write-for-at-least-an-hour-per-day regimen. And, of course, I had the unexpected side trip to the operating room and the resulting recovery from back surgery.

So how did writing this book rate for me on my personal SCALES scale? Actually, quite well—with some caveats. First, in case I haven't told you, I hate to write. After devoting over a thousand hours of effort to just the task of writing and editing of this book (not to mention the research and hands-on practice of the various pursuits), I have learned (at least) three things: 1) it still requires a significant effort and a bunch of self-cajoling to force myself to sit down and take up the electronic pen; 2) once at the keyboard the time flies; and 3) I derive a tremendous sense of accomplishment from the finished product. For me, writing is a fairly effective way to achieve Dr. Csikszentmihalyi's state of flow.

But how would writing in a generic sense rate? Probably not very well. Let's walk through the elements:

Social Interaction—When I write, my affair with the muse requires solitude and silence. Conversations with other writers confirm that I am not unique in this condition. The composition of the written word may seem to be a lonely endeavor, but a book, particularly nonfiction, involves a great deal more than just the writing. Researching the topics for the book or piece, as well as the efforts required to garner the facts, depending of course on the subject matter, may necessitate a good deal of social engagement.

In the case of this book, the various activities covered in Part II involved a great deal of outreach as I have wandered from rural churches to Rotary meetings (large and small) to bridge venues to comedy clubs. Admittedly, when I have written pieces on more esoteric (and boring) topics, such as reform of the residential mortgage finance system, social interaction has been much more limited. Perhaps I would have had the same experience if I had been trying to write the Great American Novel. The point here may be that, as with so many other situations in life, it is what you make it, and you need to be mindful of the results you hope to achieve. Thus, if you want to write and you want to include a social element, you should take that into account when you choose your topic.

With this project, there has been an added and unexpected "social interaction" perk. I have been able to turn many awkward social interactions into a kind of informal research project. Many times over the past umpteen months, when there was an uncomfortable silence in a cocktail party conversation or I was seated next to someone with whom I had only limited familiarity, I would pose an open-ended question like, "What do you do in your spare time?" or "Are you considering retirement?" or "Now that you're not working at [fill in the blank], is there anything you would do differently with your new life?" If my dinner partner was someone that I knew well enough that I thought I could get away with it, I might ask "What makes you truly happy?"

I realize that the icebreaker benefits of the subject matter of this book are somewhat unique, but my point is that there can be unexpected opportunities for social interaction even in this seemingly isolationist pastime. Hell, for that matter, I noticed that once the word got out that I was working on this book, many of my friends would go out of their way to inquire about its progress—a bit of social engagement lagniappe.

Given that I have intentionally tried to use this book to assess the benefits of writing as a possible passion to pursue, the activity garners a five in this category.

Concentration—Out of the park. Some writers have a natural talent that causes compelling paragraphs seemingly to appear on the screen in a seamless and logical flow. I haven't yet met any of those people, and I clearly don't qualify.

All the writers I have met describe writing as a labor—even when it is a labor of love—requiring significant levels of concentration. I suppose the necessary level of focus might decrease if you write on similar topics repetitively, but I haven't found that to be the case. For me, even drafting emails to my clients on familiar legal matters requires focus and concentration. No doubt, composing this book has required more, as I have wrestled with unfamiliar territory and new ideas. But I think you should get points whenever you organize your thoughts and immortalize them in a coherent fashion in writing.

The composition of the text is only part of the story. The topics covered here were by and large novel ones for me—and by "topics" I mean not just the activities to which I applied the SCALES scale. Researching the field of positive psychology, dementia, resilience, and physical health broadened my knowledge of areas that I just haven't encountered in my professional career. From the outset, I have confessed that I am not a qualified expert on any of these matters, but I certainly have a better understanding, and appreciation, of these topics now than when I started.

Whatever knowledge I have gained has been enhanced by the process of organizing my research and applying it to a challenge that many people in my purview encounter—successful retirement. But many of the principles I have covered in my research have much broader application. Initially, I had a goal of exploring post-retirement activities. That simple inquiry led me in different directions and to additional research. Each twist led to another turn, all of which required exploration and concentration. Based on all I have read and learned, I believe this is just the sort of brain stimulation that would result in a longer, saner life. Moreover, I have always found that my comprehension of subject matter improves if I have to synthesize what I am learning by putting it in writing, not to mention my retention of the information. All of this required concentration for me at the max.

A score of 10 seems appropriate on the use of my noodle as a writer.

Accomplishment—For me, this element is also a home run on the SCALES scale. As confessed in Chapter 2, writing always provides me with a sense of personal accomplishment. Up until now, the results of my efforts typically have been shorter pieces, usually of a highly technical nature. *What Now?* has required more ink to give the subjects comprehensive coverage. I honestly had to draw a line in the sand on the coverage of each of the five applications in Part II. All were enjoyable enough, and the opportunities for further challenges in each were great enough, that it was difficult to stop and move on to the next. Otherwise, I would never reach the conclusion of this chapter.

Of course, there is no logical tie between length and satisfaction of the quest for accomplishment, but I honestly believe that size matters here. The longer the writing, the more effort that has been *required*, the greater the sense of accomplishment. (Okay, okay, I recognize that you, as a reader, don't care to indulge my need for accomplishment by wading through unnecessary verbiage. That's why I have carefully pruned all the excess before you picked up the book. Trust me on this one.) As I near the end of this experiment, my subjective feeling of accomplishment is over the top—another 10.

Laughter—As with any of the pursuits I've covered here, the level of humor seems to be largely dependent on the subject matter and how you approach it. Most people, including yours truly, wouldn't think of conducting research and the production of the written word as chuckle-inducing. In fact, as I learned in my foray into stand-up comedy, even writing a stand-up routine is a great deal of work. Nevertheless, some tasks are more amusing than others.

This project has been fun, and I have had lots of laughs along the way. The topics I have chosen have been enjoyable and I have approached each, to a greater or lesser extent, from a mindset of placing enjoyment over accomplishment. In addition, I cheated a bit in the transcription of my research and experiences by adding the jokes at the end of each chapter. That habit required me to gather my (clean) favorites and try to connect them (loosely) to the topics covered. I hope you enjoyed them as much as I did.

Once again, I have to look at this factor through the lens I have chosen—this book. Accordingly, writing gets a score of six on the laughter scale.

Exercise—Nada. Let's face it—writing, in and of itself, does not involve any aerobic activities. Likewise with research. With the advent of the internet, you don't even get to walk around the stacks in the library.

As I have covered in the application of the SCALES scale to the other four possible activities I have pursued for this book, none of them required any sustained physical activity. Thus, even the participation element of my research for the writing of this book involved only mild physical exertion. I suppose you could come up with a topic that would require aerobic research. Unfortunately, I think some version of *So You Think You Want to Do the Iron Man Triathlon* has already been written.

While writing is pretty sedentary and none of the research I conducted would be considered particularly physical, I believe there is something to be said for just suiting up and showing up. If nothing else, I experienced exhaustion on many occasions as I tried out my various possible pursuits. Perhaps I am being overly generous here, but the overall process of writing this book earns an exercise score of two.

Spirituality—Similar to exercise, the degree of spirituality I experienced throughout this process has been dependent, in part, on the subject matter being covered. Sacred Harp singing, for instance, had the raw ingredients for an ongoing spiritual uplifting. Unfortunately, I was too focused on the singing to pay the necessary attention to the messages contained in the hymns. Service clubs have a clear spiritual side, if you choose to pursue it. Duplicate bridge and stand-up comedy, not so much.

A focus on the spirituality that attended the other activities falls short of a complete assessment, however. The research that caused me to come up with the SCALES scale required substantial soul-searching and self-examination. The realization of the importance of spirituality to well-being served as a reinforcement of that element in my day-to-day activities. I suppose there is an element of circularity to this line of reasoning—my activity was more spiritual because it caused me to consider the spiritual. However you want to view it, this process has involved an awakening to the importance of the second "s" in SCALES.

Moreover, few things cement inwardly looking thoughts more than taking notes and forming a coherent narrative about what you see inside. The research that introduced me to eudaemonia and positive psychology, Drs. Ryff, Seligman, Csikszentmihalyi, and Lyubomirsky, would not have made the same impression unless I had attempted to synthesize the concepts and see how they apply to my life. Writing may be a solitary endeavor, but that time alone with yourself, particularly when you are focused on self-improvement, is quality time.

Taken together, all of this suggests that writing for me has entailed a good deal of a certain kind of spirituality. By definition, this element is highly subjective, and I subjectively assign a score of eight.

Add it all up and writing the book earns a composite score of 7.2.

And then, there is also the issue of my opinion of writing. I still hate to write. But there is no doubt in my mind that it is an effective avenue for me to enter a state of flow. As I have found with other projects that have required me to put keystroke to electronic vellum over the years, composing this book has taken me into that state to which Dr. C recommends we should aspire. Once I open the laptop, I lose track of time and achieve personal satisfaction that I am producing some worthwhile work product. (You may disagree with my evaluation of this book's informational value, but you have stuck with it this far, so something must have grabbed you.)

Perhaps the lesson here for me is that I have to approach any activity with the end game in mind. If I choose to write, I need to be mindful of the subject I choose. If I want to get the most out of the endeavor from a long, happy, sane, and physically fit life standpoint, I need to choose topics that will require me to get out, learn new things, meet new people, and stretch my mind and body.

Maybe I should make a conscious effort to choose subjects where the research will require physical exertion. If I pick serious topics, I always need to look for the humorous side. And if the result of my efforts will mean others will benefit, all the better. I suspect this approach is not suitable for everyone. But it works for me. I sincerely hope you have gotten as much out of this effort as I have and, with any luck, it may help you find your flow place.

You should always keep in mind that sometimes even the best laid plans, motivated by the best of intentions, can go awry.

Three sons grew up, went out on their own, and prospered. Getting back together, they discussed the gifts they were able to give their elderly mother. The first said, "I built a big house for her."

The second said, "I sent her a Rolls Royce with a driver."

The third smiled and said, "I've got you both beat. Remember how Mom enjoyed reading the Bible? And you know she can't see very well these days. I sent her a remarkable parrot that has been trained to recite the entire Bible. It took elders in the church 12 years to teach him. He's one of a kind. Mom just has to name the chapter and verse and the parrot quotes it verbatim."

Soon thereafter, the mother sent a letter to each son. "George," she wrote one son, "the house you built is pretty but it is so huge. I live in only one room, but I have to clean the whole house."

"Jimmy," she wrote to another, "I am too old to get out much. I stay most of the time at home, so I rarely use the Rolls. And the driver is so rude!"

"Dearest Donald," she wrote to her third boy, "you have the good sense to know what your mother likes. The chicken was delicious."

Epilogue

At the beginning of this tome, I employed the analogy of comparing this planning process to a journey, and, because I'm not very creative, I'll return to it. The trip I've been on over the past couple of years has been eye-opening for a number of reasons. By getting out of my comfort zone, I have seen living, breathing examples of how vast the opportunities are for an enjoyable, challenging life outside of work. I have also come to realize that, at some point, my Type A personality needs to be redirected if I want it to work to my advantage. That realization runs contrary to a work ethic that I spent years cultivating. At some stage, it is to my long-term benefit to focus on my well-being from a different perspective.

I'm more convinced than ever that the line I heard repeated so often, "I have to keep working because it's all I know how to do," can be just a cop-out. Even for those lucky few who find their professional lives to be enjoyable and rewarding after most of their colleagues have moved on to the next stage, consideration of the alternatives is time well spent. Vast opportunities exist. All you have to do is open your eyes and look around. Jump in your mental jalopy and start your trip. It may be scary, but it's a ton of fun. More importantly, it's good for you.

To save you the trouble of remembering or flipping back through the chapters, here is a recap of the scores I came up with for the five activities to which I applied the SCALES scale:

Sacred Harp Singing	5.6
Service Club Participation	7.2
Duplicate Bridge	7.1
Stand-up Comedy	6.4
Nonfiction Writing	7.2

Some readers may criticize the depth of my dives on my coverage of one or more of these pursuits. The criticism is valid to a point. The accuracy of the scoring on the SCALES scale would likely improve with more time spent on any activity but at the expense of trying out different stuff. In fact, one of the challenges I had was drawing the line on the numbers of activities to consider and to limit the time spent on a particular subject. I kept having to say to myself that it is time to move on; otherwise, I will never finish this book. Would it have been fun to cover some of the other possible pursuits on my list? You bet it would (and maybe I will).

Then, of course, there is a question of what you should do with this data you have gathered. Is there a minimum score for continuing with an activity? Do you keep trying stuff in search of the perfect 10? What if you really enjoy some activity or another, but when you factor in the other elements, you arrive at an overall score that is lower than other less enjoyable activities?

Stop! I am not your mother, and you are too old for these self-doubts. Now, you know the rules, or, more likely, I have reminded you of some rules you already knew. So, if you really get a kick out of stamp collecting or following the Grateful Dead (or whatever passes for that band today) around the country, or whatever pastime floats your boat, and these activities have low scores in exercise or spirituality or social interaction or some other SCALES, it is up to you to figure out how to augment your passion to fill in the gaps.

After all, even the weightings in the SCALES formula itself are intended to be manipulated to take into account the likes and dislikes of the user. If you want to convince your significant other that you are pursuing a particular passion because the SCALES scale says it is good for you, be my guest. At least you know the elements that should be considered. The overarching stated goal here, of course, is to maximize your chances of leading a longer, happier, and saner life. I hope I have provided you an approach to work toward that goal. This is one of those rare cases in life where it is okay to cheat. You now know how the scale works, and you are entitled to put your thumb on it to tilt it in your favor—or not. You are in control here.

For me—so far, so good. But (with any luck) there are many more miles of road to cover. And just doing what you've always done is not only boring but also not the optimal way to cover the distance. Keep in mind—retirement from your professional career should not be the beginning of the end, just the beginning of an exciting and rewarding next leg of the trip.

I have made some important discoveries on my journey thus far that may be of interest to you. Among those tidbits:

- Successful retirement means a lot more than amassing a large 401k account.
- There is no ideal pursuit, there are no silver bullets, and there are no right or wrong answers. But there are ways to improve the odds of enjoying a long and happy post-career life, and the process of discovery is well worth the effort.
- Just saying the two words "I retire" is much harder than I ever would have imagined.
- Shifting from "saving for retirement" to "spending my retirement" requires a significant (and unexpected) change in attitude.
- Older age is not for sissies, and the older you get the harder you have to fight its effects and expect the unexpected (and unfortunate).
- The rules never really change—it just gets harder to remember them and easier to slough off the need to apply them (and you have fewer people around you in a position to require you to play by them).
- There are fascinating subcultures all around you that you've never taken the time to notice. Now, you can make the time.
- There's a reason they call them "comfort zones" (and leaving them takes more guts the older you get).
- Eyeglasses can hide in a million places, but the worst is on your forehead.
- Don't be fooled by how easy a retirement lifestyle can look from a distance. Any endeavor worth pursuing will take a lot of effort.
- 60 may be the new 40, but you can't prove it by your energy level.
- If it were easy, everybody would be doing it—and the harder it is, the more satisfying it will be when you're through.

While this list may seem trite or simplistic to you, it has been a really eye-opening trip for me so far. I've got no idea what additional lessons lie ahead, but I'm reasonably certain there will be more.

As planned, the activities I tried to examine covered a pretty large waterfront. I hope there was at least one that intrigued or even appealed you. But my intent all along has not been to convince you to take up any of these pursuits.

In fact, one of the selection criteria at the outset was to try a couple of activities that are, shall we say, offbeat. Stand-up comedy comes to mind. Instead, I have attempted to find some common goals and provide you with an easily remembered lens through which to view pastimes that you are considering. If I have also conveyed a spirit of "go ahead and give it a try, what've you got to lose, and look what you gain in the process" then I have scored the equivalent of a triple/triple in my view.

So after all of this, you may be asking: "Where did Rob land?" I guess you'll have to buy my next book to find out.

In the meantime, I'm hopeful that your road trip works out the way you have it planned.

Two women met for the first time since graduating together from high school. One asked the other, "You were always so organized in school. Did you manage to live a well-planned life?"

"Yes," said her friend. "My first marriage was to a multimillionaire; my second marriage was to an actor; my third marriage was to a preacher; and now I'm married to an undertaker."

"What do those marriages have to do with a well-planned life?"

"One for the money, two for the show, three to get ready, and four to go."

Appendix

Initial List of Possible Passions to Pursue (in no particular order)

Bed & Breakfast Operator	Affordable Housing Advocate
National Parks Explorer	Seminary
Mah Jong	Horticulture/Gardening
Sacred Harp Singing	Travel
Writing	Woodworking
Fly Fishing	Church Choir
Antique Car Collecting	Duplicate Bridge
Tai-chi	Shriners
Numismatics	Lampbuilding
Private Pilot	Farming
Treasure Hunting	Civil War Artifact Collecting
Yoga	Apiarist/Beekeeping
Golf Junkie	Welding
Motorcycle Club	Tae Kwan Do
Country Store Operator	Book Club
Genealogy	Poker
Political Discussion Group/Blog	Volunteer Work
Audit College Courses	Magic
Poetry	Hike Appalachian Trail
Day Trading	Professional Clown
Puzzler	Gliding
Civil War Battlefield Explorer	Route 66 in a '66
Stand-Up Comedian	Dog Breeding
Teaching (Law)	Birding
Snow Skiing Instructor	Gourmet Cooking

Chess
Master Swimmer/English Channel
Rotary Service
Public Radio Network Founder
Alabama Explorer
Carpentry
Bowling
Habitat for Humanity Organizer/Builder
Quilting
Stargazing/Astronomy
Circumnavigate the Globe
Certified Coin Grading
Pro Bono Criminal Defense Lawyer

Graduate Degree in History
Auto Mechanic
Tri-Athlete
Volunteer Income Tax Preparer
Angel Investing
Video Gaming
Sailing
Photography
Banjo Picking
Turkey Hunting
LEGO Enthusiast
Fleamarketing/Antiquing
AKC Dog Showing

End Notes

Chapter 1. Why Are You Reading This?

1. Jen Sincero, *You Are a Badass: How to Stop Doubting Your Greatness and Start Living an Awesome Life* (Philadelphia: Running Press, 2013).
2. Franca, 2009.
3. Mark van Vugt, "Laughter Really Is the Best Medicine," *Psychology Today*, posted October 5, 2012, https://www.psychologytoday.com/blog/naturally-selected/201210/laughter-really-is-the-best-medicine.
4. Social Security Administration, *Retirement & Survivors Benefits: Life Expectancy Calculator*, https://www.ssa.gov/cgi-bin/longevity.cgi.
5. Centers for Disease Control and Prevention: National Center for Health Statistics, *Mortality in the United States, 2015*, https://www.cdc.gov/nchs/products/databriefs/db267.htm.
6. SmartAsset, "The Retirement Age in Every State in 2015," https://smartasset.com/retirement/average-retirement-age-in-every-state.

Chapter 2. Just Do What Makes You Happy

7. *Aristotle: Nicomachean Ethics*, Book I, Chapters 4 and 5.
8. Tom Butler-Bowdon, "Spiritual Classics," review of Al-Ghazali, *The Alchemy of Happiness* (1097).
9. Carol Ryff, "Happiness Is Everything, or Is It? Explorations on the Meaning of Psychological Well-being," *Journal of Personality and Social Psychology*, 57, No. 6 (1989), 1069-1081. See also Carol Ryff, "Psychological Well-being Revisited: Advances in the Science and Practice of Eudaimonia," *Psychology and Psychosomatics*, 83, no. 1 (2014).
10. A. H. Maslow, "A Theory of Human Motivation," *Psychological Review*, 50 (1943), pp. 370-396.
11. Gregg Henriques, "Six Domains of Psychological Well-being: Ryff's Six Domains of Psychological Well-being," *Psychology Today*, posted May 15, 2014, https://www.psychologytoday.com/blog/theory-knowledge/201405/six-domains-psychological-well-being.
12. Martin Seligman, *Flourish: A Visionary New Understanding of Happiness and Well-being* (New York: Free Press, 2011).

[13] Martin Seligman, *Authentic Happiness: Using the New Positive Psychology to Realize Your Potential for Lasting Fulfillment* (New York: Simon and Schuster, 2002). Seligman's PERMA approach serves as the thrust of an entire department at the University of Pennsylvania, which you can access at https://www.authentichappiness.sas.upenn.edu/learn.

[14] Barbara Bradley Hagerty, *Life Reimagined: The Science, Art, and Opportunity of Midlife* (New York: Riverhead Books), p. 272.

[15] Mihaly Csikszentmihalyi, *Flow: The Psychology of Optimal Experience* (New York: Harper Perennial, 1990).

[16] Maslow, A Theory of Human Motivation, *Psychological Review*.

[17] Definition of Flow, Wikipedia Encyclopedia, last modified December 2, 2017, https://en.wikipedia.org/wiki/Flow_(psychology).

[18] Mihaly Csikszentmihalyi, TED Talk, April 14, 2015, https://www.npr.org/2015/04/17/399806632/what-makes-a-life-worth-living.

[19] Sonja Lyubomirsky, *The How of Happiness: A New Approach to Getting the Life You Want* (New York: Penguin Group, 2007).

[20] Lyubomirsky, *The How of Happiness*, pp. 2, 25.

[21] Lyubomirsky, *The How of Happiness*, p. 39.

[22] Lyubomirsky, *The How of Happiness*, pp. 88-254.

[23] Lyubomirsky, *The How of Happiness*, pp. 84-86.

[24] Martin Seligman, *Flourish: A Visionary New Understanding of Happiness and Well-being* (New York: Free Press, 2011).

[25] https://www.authentichappiness.sas.upenn.edu/testcenter

Chapter 3. I'm Driving Me Crazy

[26] Alliance for Aging Research, Silverbook, 2015 http://www.silverbook.org/fact/growth-of-65-population-between-2003-and-2060/.

[27] Alzheimer's Association, 2016 Alzheimer's Disease Facts and Figures, "Alzheimer's & Dementia," p. 23.

[28] Alzheimer's Association, 2016 Facts and Figures, 45. See also National Institutes of Health, "Sustaining Momentum: NIH Takes Aim at Alzheimer's Disease & Related Dementias," 2017, p. 4, https://www.nia.nih.gov/sites/default/files/2017-07/FY19-bypass-budget-report-508_0.pdf.

[29] Alzheimer's Association, 2016 Facts and Figures, p. 45.

[30] Kenneth Langa, *et al.*, "A Comparison of the Prevalence of Dementia in the United States in 2000 and 2012," *Journal of the American Medical Association*, 2016, http://jamanetwork.com/journals/jamainternalmedicine/article-abstract-/2587084.

31. Ginis, BMC Public Health, 2017; https://www.sciencedaily.com/releases/2017/05/170516124023.htm.
32. The National Academies of Sciences, Engineering, and Medicine and the Agency for Healthcare Research and Quality, "Preventing Cognitive Decline and Dementia: A Way Forward," June 2017, http://nationalacademies.org/hmd/reports/2017/preventing-cognitive-decline-and-dementia-a-way-forward.aspx.
33. Deepak Chopra and Rudolph Tanzi, *Super Brain: Unleashing the Explosive Power of Your Mind to Maximize Health, Happiness, and Spiritual Well-Being* (New York: Harmony Books), p. 30.
34. National Academies and AHRQ, "Preventing Cognitive Decline," p. 5.
35. Savordo, Stroke and Neuroplasticity, *Periodicum Biologorum*, 2012.
36. Hagerty, *Life Reimagined*, p. 126, citing P. A. Boyle, et al., "Effect of a Purpose in Life on Risk of Incident Alzheimer's Disease and Mild Cognitive Impairment in Community-Dwelling Older Persons," *Archives of General Psychiatry*, 67, No. 3 (2010), pp. 304-310.
37. Edward Taub, et al., "Plasticity in the Motor System Related to Therapy-Induced Improvement of Movement After Stroke," *NeuroReport*, 10, No. 4 (March 17, 1999), pp. 807–810. See also Iris Zavoreo, et al., "Stroke and Neuroplasticity," *Periodicum Biologorum*, 114, No. 3 (2012), pp. 393-396.
38. Blundon, http://science.sciencemag.org/content/356/6345/1352.
39. David Snowdon, "Aging and Alzheimer's Disease: Lessons from the Nun Study," *The Gerontologist*, 37, No. 2 (1997): pp. 150-156; School Sisters of Notre Dame, "Nun Study," last accessed December 11, 2017, http://ssnd.org/ministries/nun_study/#.WjAPoUqnHIU.
40. "The Nun Study," University of Minnesota, https://www.healthstudies.umn.edu/nunstudy/. "What Science Learned from a Group of Elderly Nuns," *Introductory Statistics*, January 28, 2011.
41. 2016 Alzheimer's Disease Facts and Figures, p. 13.
42. National Academies and AHRQ, "Preventing Cognitive Decline," pp. 7-8.
43. WebMD, "Alzheimer's Disease Health Center: Brain Exercises and Dementia," last accessed December 11, 2017, https://www.webmd.com/alzheimers/guide/preventing-dementia-brain-exercises#1.
44. Chopra and Tanzi, *Super Brain*, pp. 40-41.

Chapter 4. Spirituality
45. HealthCommunities.com, "Healthy Aging: Health Benefits of Spirituality," last modified July 27, 2013, http://www.healthcommunities.com/healthy-aging/spirituality-health-benefits.shtml.

[46] *The Holy Bible: Containing the Old and New Testaments in the King James Version*, Matthew 23:5 (Nashville: Thomas Nelson, 1984). The term "phylacteries" refers to small, black leather cubes containing a piece of parchment inscribed with verses from the Old Testament.

[47] Matthew 5:15.

[48] Thich Hanh, *Living Buddha, Living Christ* (New York: Penguin Publishing Group, 1995), pp. 16-18.

[49] Seppälä, *Psychology Today*, Aug. 8, 2016.

[50] Lyubomirsky, *The How of Happiness*, p. 232.

[51] Pew Research Center, "Highly Religious People Not Distinctive in All Aspects of Everyday Life," April 12, 2016, http://www.pewforum.org/2016/04/12/highly-religious-people-not-distinctive-in-all-aspects-of-everyday-life/. See also Emma Seppälä, "The Surprising Health Benefits of Spirituality," *Psychology Today*, posted August 8, 2016, https://www.psychologytoday.com/blog/feeling-it/201608/the-surprising-health-benefits-spirituality.

[52] Chopra and Tanzi, *Super Brain*, p. 282.

Chapter 5. I've Got Friends in Flow Places

[53] Sinclair Lewis, *Babbitt* (New York: Brace & Co., 1922).

[54] Harvard Study of Adult Development, http://www.adultdevelopmentstudy.org/. See also "Good Genes Are Nice, but Joy Is Better," *Harvard Gazette*, April 11, 2017, https://news.harvard.edu/gazette/story/2017/04/over-nearly-80-years-harvard-study-has-been-showing-how-to-live-a-healthy-and-happy-life/.

[55] Robert Waldinger, TED Talk, November 2015, https://www.ted.com/talks/robert_waldinger_what_makes_a_good_life_lessons_from_the_longest_study_on_happiness.

[56] Mihaly Csikszentmihalyi, review of "Finding Flow," *Psychology Today*, 2016.

[57] Social Relationships and Health: A Flashpoint, p. 2.

[58] Social Media Update 2016, http://www.pewinternet.org/2016/11/11/social-media-update-2016/.

[59] https://womhealth.org.au/healthy-lifestyle/health-benefits-social-media.

[60] Margalit, https://www.psychologytoday.com/blog/behind-online-behavior/201408/the-psychology-behind-social-media-interactions.

[61] Margalit, https://www.psychologytoday.com/blog/behind-online-behavior/201408/the-psychology-behind-social-media-interactions.

[62] Umberson, *et al.* 2006.

[63] American Society on Aging, Survey of Research on Social Relationships.

End Notes

64 Chris Crowley and Henry Lodge, *Younger Next Year* (New York: Workman Publishing, 2004), p. 47.
65 Cohen, *Social Relationships and Health*, p. 678.
66 Daniel DeNoon, *Harvard Health Blog*, Harvard Medical School, "A Dog Could Be Your Heart's Best Friend," posted May 22, 2013, https://www.health.harvard.edu/blog/a-dog-could-be-your-hearts-best-friend-201305226291.
67 *Berkeley Wellness*, University of California-Berkeley, "Can Pets Help You Live Longer?" posted November 29, 2013, http://www.berkeleywellness.com/self-care/preventive-care/article/can-pets-help-you-live-longer.

Chapter 6. Oh No! Not Another Infomercial about Exercise

68 Office of Disease Prevention and Health Promotion, "Physical Activity Guidelines," Chap. 2, last accessed December 14, 2017, https://health.gov/paguidelines/guidelines/chapter2.aspx.
69 Gretchen Reynolds, "A Fitness Check at Your Checkup," *The New York Times*, December 12, 2016.
70 American Heart Association, "Recommendations for Physical Activities in Adults," last accessed December 15, 2017, http://www.heart.org/HEARTORG/HealthyLiving/PhysicalActivity/FitnessBasics/American-Heart-Association-Recommendations-for-Physical-Activity-in-Adults_UCM_307976_Article.jsp#.
71 OHPDP, "Physical Activity Guidelines," https://health.gov/paguidelines/guidelines/chapter2.aspx.

Chapter 7. Have You Heard the One About...

72 Michael Miller, University of Maryland Medical Center, "University of Maryland School of Medicine Study Shows Laughter Helps Blood Vessels Function Better," *ScienceDaily*, 19 March 2005, www.sciencedaily.com/releases/2005/03/050309111444.htm.
73 Mayo Clinic, "Healthy Lifestyle: Stress Management," last updated April 21, 2016, https://www.mayoclinic.org/healthy-lifestyle/stress-management/in-depth/stress-relief/art-20044456?pg=2&p=1.
74 Irene Hatzipapas, Maretha Visser, and Estie van Rensburg, "Laughter Therapy as an Intervention to Promote Psychological Well-being of Volunteer Community Care Workers Working with HIV-Affected Families," *Journal of Social Aspects of HIV/Aids* 14, No. 1, 2017.
75 Elizabeth Scott, "The Stress Management and Health Benefits of Laughter," *verywell*, last updated April 17, 2017, https://www.verywell.com/the-stress-management-and-health-benefits-of-laughter-3145084.

76. Lawrence Robinson, Melinda Smith, and Jeanne Segal, "Laughter is the Best Medicine," *HelpGuide*, last updated October, 2017, https://www.helpguide.org/articles/mental-health/laughter-is-the-best-medicine.htm.
77. Scott, "Stress Management."
78. Mayo Clinic, "Stress Management."
79. Tamara Lechner, "Six Reasons Why Laughter Is the Best Medicine," 2016, http://www.chopra.com/articles/6-reasons-why-laughter-is-the-best-medicine#sm.0000d7s2ale5zdwnzf71k7on38bv2.
80. Michele Tugade, Barbara Fredrickson, and Lisa Barrett, "Psychological Resilience and Positive Emotional Granularity: Examining the Benefits of Positive Emotions on Coping and Health," National Center for Biotechnology Information, 2005, https://www.ncbi.nlm.nih.gov/pmc/articles/PMC1201429/.
81. Aaron O'Banion and Justin Bashore, "He Who Laughs Most is Most Likely to Last," 2017, Social Anxiety Institute, https://socialanxietyinstitute.org/he-who-laughs-most.
82. Markham Heid, "You Asked: Does Laughing Have Real Health Benefits?" Time.com, November 19, 2014, http://time.com/3592134/laughing-health-benefits.
83. GS Bains, *et al.*, "The Effect of Humor on Short-term Memory in Older Adults: A New Component for Whole-person Wellness," National Center for Biotechnology Information (2014), https://www.ncbi.nlm.nih.gov/pmc/articles/PMC1201429/.
84. Robert Provine, *Laughter: A Scientific Investigation* (New York: Penguin Books, 2000).

Chapter 8. Resilience, or No Excuses

85. Robert Cummings and Mark Wooden, "Personal Resilience in Times of Crisis: The Implications of SWB Homeostasis and Set-Points," *Journal of Happiness Studies* 15, No. 1, 2014, p. 10.
86. Cummings and Wooden, "Personal Resilience," p. 1.
87. National Multiple Sclerosis Society, *Resilience: Addressing the Challenges of MS*, last accessed December 16, 2017, https://www.nationalmssociety.org/Resources-Support/Library-Education-Programs/Resilience-Addressing-The-Challenges-Of-MS.
88. See also Michele Tugade, *et al.*, "Psychological Resilience and Positive Emotional Granularity: Examining the Benefits of Positive Emotions on Coping and Health," *Journal of Personality*, 72, No. 6, 2004, pp. 1161–1190.
89. See Karen Reivich, *et al.* (2011), "Master Resilience Training in the U.S. Army," *American Psychologist* 66, No.1, 2011, pp. 25-34.
90. United States Department of the Army, Army Regulation 350-53, *Comprehensive Soldier and Family Fitness*, effective June 19, 2014.
91. Hara Marano, "The Art of Resilience," *Psychology Today*, last reviewed June 9, 2016, https://www.psychologytoday.com/articles/200305/the-art-resilience.

[92] Kramer, "The Resilience Factor," *Momentum Magazine*, 2016.
[93] Southwick and Charney, "Resilience: The Science of Mastering Life's Greatest Challenges" (Cambridge, UK: Cambridge University Press, 2012).
[94] Liam Graham and Andrew Oswald, "Hedonic Capital, Adaptation and Resilience," *Journal of Economic Behavior and Organization* (2010).
[95] Cristiane Nalin and Lucia Franca, "The Importance of Resilience for Well-being in Retirement," *Paideia* 25, No. 61, 2015, p. 192.

Chapter 9. Pulling It All Together
[96] Hagerty, *Life Reimagined*, 79.

Chapter 10. Heading for Hayden
[97] B. F. White and E. J. King, *The Sacred Harp* (1844).
[98] Hugh McGraw, *et al.*, eds., *The Sacred Harp* (Sacred Harp Publishing Company, Inc., 1991), p. 14.
[99] McGraw, *et al.*, *The Sacred Harp*, p. 15.
[100] McGraw, *et al.*, *The Sacred Harp*, p. 45.
[101] McGraw, *et al.*, *The Sacred Harp*, p. 98.

Chapter 11. Heading for Harbert
[102] Alexis de Tocqueville, *Democracy in America* (New York: G. Adlard, 1839).
[103] Corporation for National and Community Service, "Volunteering and Civic Life in America," last accessed December 16, 2017, https://www.nationalservice.gov/vcla.
[104] Robert Putnam, "The Strange Disappearance of Civic America," *The American Prospect* (No. 24, 1996), http://prospect.org/article/strange-disappearance-civic-america.
[105] Quentin Wodon, "Rotary Membership Analysis 2: The Challenge," *Rotarian Economist* (2014), https://rotarianeconomist.com/2014/12/22/rotary-membership-analysis-2-the-challenge/.
[106] For a current glimpse of the services being offered by the Cancer Prevention and Early Detection Center in Colombo, Sri Lanka, go to http://www.nccp.health.gov.lk/index.php/menu-styles/main-menu.

Chapter 12. Heading for Hoover
[107] American Contract Bridge League, "Learn to Play Bridge," last accessed December 15, 2017, http://www.acbl.org/learn_page/.
[108] Jeanne Wamack, *Building Bridges* (2016).

[109] ACBL, "Masterpoint Awards Chart," last accessed December 17, 2017, http://www.acbl.org/clubs_page/club-administration/resources-and-forms/masterpoint-awards-chart/.

[110] You wouldn't be reading this endnote unless you don't believe my math. I'll admit the number is mind-boggling, but I didn't make that number up. The University of Kansas Math Department has a great explanation at https://www.math.ku.edu/~jmartin/bridge/basics.pdf.

Chapter 13. Heading for Hoover—the Sequel

[111] "Inside the Brutal World of Comedy Open Mikes," *The New York Times*, 2/17/2017.

Chapter 15. Heading for Hoover—the Sequel (continued)

[112] Amy Schumer, *The Girl with the Lower Back Tattoo* (New York: Gallery Books, 2016), p. 151.

[113] Apatow, *Sick in the Head* (New York: Random House, 2015), p. 5.

[114] Apatow, *Sick in the Head*, p. 156.

[115] Apatow, *Sick in the Head*, p. 161.

[116] Apatow, *Sick in the Head*, p. 126.

[117] Robert Provine, "The Science of Laughter," *Psychology Today*, last revised June 9, 2016, https://www.psychologytoday.com/articles/200011/the-science-laughter.

[118] Greg Dean, *Step by Step to Stand-up Comedy* (Portsmouth: Heinemann, 2000).

Kathryn Gaiennie Photography

About the Author

Rob Couch was born and raised in Texarkana, Texas/Arkansas. After attending both undergraduate and law schools at Washington & Lee University, he settled in Birmingham, Alabama. He has spent 40 years working in accounting, law, commercial banking, mortgage banking, and government. He currently lives at home in Birmingham with his wife, Anne. They have two married daughters and a grandson.

Made in the USA
Lexington, KY
20 February 2019